The History of
TORTURE
and
EXECUTION

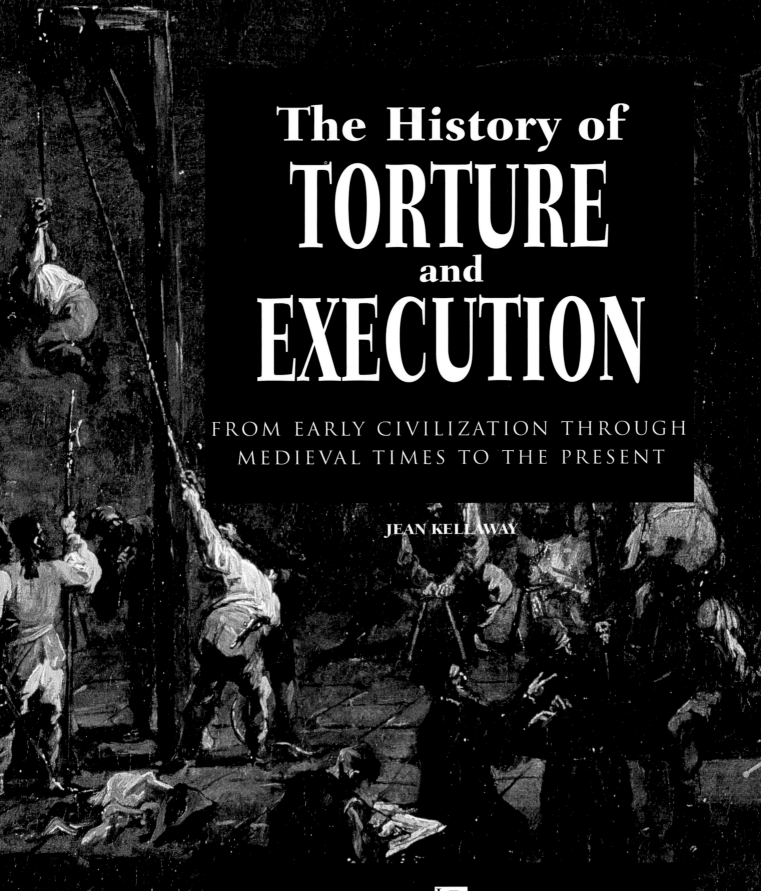

The History of
TORTURE
and
EXECUTION

FROM EARLY CIVILIZATION THROUGH
MEDIEVAL TIMES TO THE PRESENT

JEAN KELLAWAY

THE LYONS PRESS
Guilford, Connecticut
An Imprint of The Globe Pequot Press

Printed in China

ISBN-13: 978-1-58574-622-4
ISBN-10: 1-58574-622-3

Project editor: Warren Lapworth
Interior design: Paul Chubb/Thalamus Studios
Illustrations: Oliver Frey
Repro/four-color separations: Prima Media Ltd.

CONTENTS

INTRODUCTION

The progress of mankind has been shadowed by the grisly history of torture and execution. For every shining triumph of human endeavor there has been a dark example of state-sanctioned depravity. Each illustration of courage and wisdom goes hand in hand with an unbecoming horror of human design.

From the earliest known legal code, drawn up by the Babylonian king Hammurabi in the 18th century BC, capital punishment has been used both for retribution and as a deterrent. While it was astonishingly tolerant for its day, insisting that every man was equal before the law, the Code of Hammurabi—literally engraved in stone—had elements of the "eye for an eye" principle of justice.

In the Bible the death penalty is applied to more than 30 different offenses; the ancient Greeks went further still, demanding death for most misdemeanors.

The callous disregard for human life was not universal. In England King Canute and William the Conqueror were reluctant to employ the death penalty, although torture was applied.

TERRORISM AND REVENGE

But life was barbarously grim in the Middle Ages. Those in authority sought new and different ways of making an impression on an increasingly brutalized population. Zealots tried to defend their religious territories by terrorizing the faithful. Politicians and priests went to greater lengths than ever to attract the attention of the people, and were frequently guided by ritual and superstition in the process, resulting in more death and human destruction through torture.

Efforts at reform did not occur until the 18th century, when execution rates peaked in Europe. At first there was only limited success, but new philosophies gradually inspired greater understandings, amid blood-soaked spectacles such as the French Revolution. The great thinkers began to investigate their emotions—and those of the mob—when an execution was exacted. They found that vengeance was not a pretty sight.

Sir Francis Bacon commented 400 years ago that "Revenge is a kind of wild justice which the more man's nature runs to, the more ought law to weed it out."

He is in agreement with Albert Pierrepoint, the British hangman until 1956. In his biography, *Executioner Pierrepoint*, he concludes: "The fruit of my experience has this bitter after-taste; that I do not now believe that any one of the hundreds of executions I carried out has in any way acted as a deterrent against future murder. Capital punishment, in my view, achieved nothing except revenge."

EARLY CIVILIZATIONS

The classical civilizations of Greece and Rome, together with the religious legacies of the Holy Land, have shaped much of Western society. We tend to think of these cultures as nurturing great artists, inventors, writers, philosophers, orators, and military strategists. Here the seeds of democracy were sown.

Yet history shows this was also an age of despots and fanatics, ruthless leaders who saw life as cheap and power the ultimate possession. For every benevolent king who attempted rule by consensus, there were countless more who relied on fear to boost their position and stifle opposition. For them, torture and execution sent a clear warning to the masses that rebellion had its price.

In societies where death was touted as a public spectacle. these sentiments were easy to enforce. Stoning allowed everyone to play the executioner. The Egyptian pharaohs bluntly advertised their intention to decapitate opponents.

Romans delighted in the sight of a Christian ripped apart by wild animals or the blood of some hapless gladiator spilled in a glaring mismatch. Curiously, Roman spectators sometimes made moral distinctions, in one instance expressing disquiet when naked Christian women were exposed to wild beasts, seemingly because the women were mothers.

Roman emperors such as Caligula and Nero, or Greek tyrants like Phalarus or Nabis, cared little for such sentiments. For these sadistic leaders, ingenious methods of torture were an interesting distraction from the day-to-day affairs of state. Nero used live Christians as burning torches to light his garden and Phalarus's "brazen bull" turned execution into macabre entertainment. The infliction of pain and suffering was limited only by a torturer's imagination.

RIGHT: Christian martyrs pray as they are boiled in oil by Roman persecutors. Emperors such as Nero and Maximinus delighted in cruel methods of execution, as did many tyrants of the era.

DEATH BY THE NILE

The sophisticated hierarchy and structure of ancient Egypt included a fair trial and punishment system. But execution was still the ultimate penalty.

RIGHT: This decorative ax was used for one of the preferred methods of execution in ancient Egypt: beheading.

Ancient Egypt had arguably the most stable and successful civilization the world has known. Since the decipherment of the Rosetta Stone—effectively a hieroglyphics crib sheet—knowledge of its religion, government, and legal practice has increased enormously. Nonetheless, given that ancient Egyptian culture spanned more than 5,000 years, gaps in knowledge are inevitable.

The execution of servants as part of funerary rituals is one unresolved issue. Egyptologists are clear that this practice would have occurred only during the Archaic Period (c.3100–2755 BC), but the strongest supporting evidence—the royal cemetery at Abydos—is inconclusive. Archeologists found large numbers of personal servants, court officials, and concubines buried alongside their kings. It is possible that benevolent rulers made burial provisions for staff dying naturally, but the more likely scenario is that these commoners were slaughtered or forced to take poison.

It used to be thought the pyramids could only have been built by a massive labor force literally worked to death. We now know there were few slaves in Egypt's Old Kingdom and no superior weaponry with which the ruling elite could subjugate so many people. Pyramid-building was probably an act of citizenship by willing volunteers.

The Egyptian legal system was sophisticated and, at least during the rule of strong dynasties, free of corruption. It was based on a hierarchy that rose from a town or village counsel of elders (a *seru*), to regional courts in the *nomes* (administrative districts) and national high courts (*Kenbet*). There was no distinction of rank; noblemen and commoners were afforded the same opportunities.

THROWN TO THE DOGS

Capital punishment could be handed down by both regional judges and the *Kenbet*, as well as the supervising vizier. There were various state-sanctioned methods of execution, among them hanging, beheading, and strangulation. Death by burning was thought to destroy the condemned's *ba*—the human-headed bird that represented the soul. In death it was considered vital for the ba to unite with the deceased's *ka*, or spirit partner.

Political malcontents were constantly reminded of the power of the king. A damaged boundary marker placed by a royal gold mining expedition at Kurgus, on the Nile, proclaims the following warning from Thutmose I: "If any Nubian oversteps the decree which my father Amun has given to me, [his head] shall be chopped off… for me… and he shall have no heirs."

Adultery was considered a terrible crime. Women were perceived as temptresses who lured away weak but essentially innocent men. The *Westcar Papyrus*, a series of stories about King Khufu's regime (25–28 BC), records how a cheating wife was

burned alive, her ashes scattered on the Nile. Other folk stories tell of unfaithful wives being killed and thrown to dogs to eat. The Greek historian Siculus, writing in the first century BC, claimed that adulterous Egyptian women had their noses cut off.

The priest Natsef-Amun, who worked in the Great Temple of Karnak at Thebes 3,000 years ago, was mummified with his mouth open and tongue protruding, which suggests he was strangled. While it was not unknown for priests to be executed, there is no tell-tale damage to the delicate hyoid bone in his neck; his body is preserved but the cause and reason of death remain unknown.

TOP RIGHT: Egyptian burial chambers unearthed by treasure-hunters have contained the bodies of servants, as well as pharaohs and their burial goods.

ABOVE: Stories have been told of sacrifices cast into the Nile to appease the gods when the river's life-giving waters ran low.

TYRANNY OF THE GREEKS

Before Athens emerged as a powerful, democratic city-state, the Aegean's political map was dominated by tyrants. If the accounts of later classical historians are true, these dictators reveled in the design of horrifying tortures and executions.

The Greek satirist Lucian, who lived in the second century AD, described a torture machine known as the brazen bull, invented by a man named Perilaus for the entertainment of the despot Phalaris. It consisted of a life-size hollow, wooden bull, with a small door at the back. The unfortunate victim was forced to climb in, while a fire was lit beneath the beast's belly. A complex arrangement of pipes in the head converted the wretch's cries of agony into melodious music, as though the fake bull were lowing.

Lucian tells the story as though he were Phalaris, awaiting a test-run of the contraption: " 'Well now, Perilaus,' I said, 'if you are so sure of your contrivance, give us proof of it on the spot: mount up and get in and imitate the cries of a man tortured in it, that we may hear whether such charming music will proceed from it, as you make us believe.' Perilaus obeyed, and no sooner was he in the belly of the bull than I shut the aperture, and put fire beneath it." The story ends with Phalaris pulling the inventor out of the bull, "that the noble work should not be contaminated by his dying" and ordering Perilaus to be thrown to his death.

HUGGED TO DEATH

Polybius recounts an equally dastardly device, reminiscent of the "virgin's kiss" later used in medieval Germany and supposedly by the Spanish Inquisition. It was a wooden effigy of Agepa, wife of the tyrant Nabis, which was studded with sharp iron spikes concealed by clothes. The model's spring-loaded mechanism trapped the torture victim and "hugged" him increasingly tightly. It's main use, Polybius claimed, was to persuade noblemen and wealthy citizens to give more money for Nabis's coffers. Occasionally victims took small measures of revenge. The philosopher Zeno of Elea cracked under torture after his coup attempt against the ruler Niarchos failed. Zeno told his jailers that he would name his accomplices and Niarchos was summoned to the chamber. Bending low to hear the anguished man's whisper, Zeno bit off Niarchos's ear.

Similarly, Hieronymos believed he had finally broken a conspirator named Theodore after having the man flogged, stretched on the rack, and branded with red-hot irons. Ordered to identify his leader, Theodore gave the name of Hieronymos's most trusted lieutenant, who was summarily executed. Only later did the outraged ruler realize he had been fooled. By the fifth century BC Athens had emerged as a vibrant democracy in which even the poor could hold positions of power. This is not to say it was a just society by our standards. Foreigners and slaves had no legal standing and could be tortured by the courts, and were even used as torture substitutes, enduring the suffering on behalf of their masters.

THE TRIAL OF SOCRATES

The most famous execution in Athens was that of the philosopher Socrates, tried in 399 BC on charges of "neglecting established gods" and "corrupting the morals of the young." Socrates was probably seen as the instigator of an aristocratic backlash against democracy and was found guilty by a jury angered at his flippant regard of the death sentence. He refused to cooperate with an escape plan hatched by his followers and calmly drank the poisonous hemlock brew—the standard form of state execution.

BELOW: A victim is fed into a brazen bull, while Phalaris waits to hear the burning victim's cries transform into the bellows of a wild beast.

MARTYRS OF THE ARENA

As the once-mighty Roman Empire entered terminal decline, desperate emperors bolstered support with the kind of persecution tactics beloved by despots throughout history.

C hristians, with their weird beliefs and behavior, were perfect targets for the Romans. It was easy for the state to manipulate opinion against Christians for political expediency, usually in times of civil unrest. Some magistrates saw themselves as merciful and gave the religious rebels opportunities to renounce their God by making a sacrifice to the emperor's health or sprinkling incense above a lighted flame. Other Christians were tortured.

It was beyond the pagan Roman's reasoning that simple acts of sacrifice could be refused in preference to public death in the gladiatorial arena, or a mauling by wild animals. Nonetheless, Christians with strong faith defied the law and prepared for their terrible fate.

The arena mob bayed for blood. They saw Christians as dangerous scum, well-deserving of a painful death, and demanded that they suffer fear and humiliation in the process.

One of the most graphic accounts of execution by wild beasts concerned a young mother called Perpetua, a convert to Christianity, whose influential family lived near Carthage. Perpetua was in breach of laws imposed by the emperor Septimius Severus in AD 202 that allowed long-standing Christians to pursue their faith but imposed the death penalty on anyone who converted.

She was hauled before a magistrate with several of her male and female Christian slaves and two male converts. All were condemned to death in the arena in the presence of the acting governor, Halerian, as a curtain-raiser for games to celebrate the birthday of Severus's son, Geta.

MAULED BY BEASTS

Contemporary accounts show that one of the young men, Saturninus, was first to die; mauled by a leopard and savaged by a bear. Next the condemned group's teacher Saturus was sent in, tied to a boar that trampled and dragged him but returned him to his jailer alive. Saturus pleaded for a leopard to be released so that death would come quickly. As the animal tore at his limbs, the crowd reportedly taunted him with cries of "You've really been washed now," a reference to the ritual of baptism.

Perpetua, who according to Christian chroniclers entered the arena warning Halerian, "You may judge us now, but God will judge you later," was stripped naked, along with her slave girl Felicitas, wrapped in a net and exposed to the beasts.

This spectacle proved too much even for the sadistic crowd. The arena authorities allowed the women to be dressed and instead tried to kill them with a wild cow.

When this too failed gladiators were sent in to deliver the *coup de grâce*. It was said that Perpetua's executioner was inexperienced and failed to dispatch her cleanly. Crying out in agony, she guided the point of his blade to her throat, ensuring that he would not repeat his error.

LEFT: Christians cast into the arena are trampled by a rampaging horde of wild animals. Spectators generally preferred grisly, violent deaths.

NERO'S FIRE
The most notorious of Christian persecutions occurred in AD 64 when Nero decided to scotch rumors that he had deliberately burnt down a large area of Rome by blaming the fire on followers of the new religion. Whether or not this was true remains a matter of conjecture, but Nero began a genocidal program in which Christians were crucified, thrown to wild beasts, and even burnt as human torches to light the garden of his private residence, the Golden House.

STONING

In Biblical times death by stoning was a standard form of punishment laid down in the Mosaic Code, a definitive set of laws covering civil, criminal, and religious transgressions. Many Old Testament passages refer to the punishment.

The Mosaic Code appeared in the Old Testament books of Exodus, Leviticus, Numbers, and Deuteronomy, and greatly expanded the range of crimes punishable by death under Hebrew Scriptures. Stoning seems to have been regarded as particularly appropriate for sexual crimes and witchcraft. It was also the punishment for rebellious children, worshipping false gods, and working on the Sabbath.

There are many specific references. Leviticus 20:27 demands death by stoning for all mediums caught communicating with the dead. Deuteronomy lists it as the punishment for adultery, incest, and bestiality, though the idea that it was a general penalty for homosexuality is now largely discredited. Leviticus 20:13 warns: "If a man also lie with mankind, as he lieth with a woman, both of them have committed an abomination: they shall surely be put to death." This passage, together with a similar verse (Deuteronomy 22:24), is thought to refer specifically to homosexual temple prostitution, a widespread vice among many tribes bordering the Israelites.

For a woman the fear of execution depended heavily on her sexual status. A woman presented as a virgin to her husband but subsequently proved to have had sex before her engagement would face the following fate, according to Deuteronomy 22:13-21: "Then they shall bring out the damsel to the door of her father's house and the men of her city shall stone her with stones that she die...." Seemingly women were not penalized if they admitted their loss of virginity. Men were not punished for pre-marital sex. Similarly, women who allowed themselves to be seduced by one man while engaged to another risked a stoning; engaged men faced no penalty for unfaithfulness.

STONING THE REBELLIOUS

Biblical law occasionally seems an odd cocktail of generalizations and tortuous detail. For instance, Deuteronomy 21:18–21 orders that "If a man have a stubborn and rebellious son, which will not obey the voice of his father, or the voice of his mother... all the men of his city will stone him with stones, that he die." There was ambiguity in the translation from the original text so it may be that death was not intended. Nevertheless, there is no guidance as to what is "stubborn and rebellious," so the scope for interpretation is frightening.

In contrast, Exodus 21:22–23 goes into detail about what should happen in the event that a fight between men accidentally injures a pregnant woman, causing her to miscarry. It suggests remedies—depending on the woman's subsequent health—and sets out capital punishments in the event of her death. These are stoning, impaling (on a stake), and burning.

Jewish law stated that any criminal sentenced to death by stoning should be taken to a nominated place outside the city walls, where his or her accuser would throw

STONING IN IRAN

Women are still stoned to death in Iran today, in the name of Islam. Married people found guilty of adultery are buried in rocks, but men are only buried up to their neck; women are covered to the neck. Contrary to their law, those few women who free themselves are often recaptured and stoned again or immediately killed.

the first stone, after which the rest of the crowd could join in. This form of execution was maintained by the Jews for many years and was used against Saint Stephen after he was found guilty of blasphemy in hailing Jesus of Nazareth as God.

There is a danger in viewing historic laws with modern attitudes, heightened by the risk of mistranslation and misinterpretation. In defense of ancient Israel's laws, it should be stressed that the courts demanded overwhelming levels of proof before pronouncing the death penalty.

BELOW: A blasphemer staggers as "justice" is meted out with a hail of stones.

CRUCIFIXION

The link between Christ and crucifixion is theologically vital, symbolizing the very essence of Christianity. Yet Jesus was one of literally thousands who endured this agonizing execution.

Crucifixion was a common form of punishment between the 6th century BC and the 4th century AD, fit for the most lowly and reviled criminals. It was, for example, the fate of captured followers of Spartacus, the rebel gladiator who waged war on the Roman Empire some 60 years before the birth of Christ.

Flavius Josephus (AD 38–100), a Jewish diarist and historian, mentions the affecting sight of rows of crosses bearing bodies during his travels with Roman overlords: "I saw many captives crucified and remembered three of them as my former acquaintances. I was very sorry at this in my mind and went with tears in my eyes to Titus and told him of them; so he immediately commanded them to be taken down and to have the greatest care taken of them in order to their recovery; yet two of them died under the physicians hands while the third recovered." Proof, if any were needed, that a spell on the cross caused grievous injury and suffering before death prevailed.

Josephus recorded that significant numbers of crucifixions were ordered by Syria's Antiochus IV during the Jewish Maccabean revolt in 167 BC and by the Maccabeans themselves in conflict with the Pharisees 60 years later. The ruthless Syrian king had the sons of victims hung around their necks as they gasped their last. Maccabean king Alexander Jannaeus ordered his men to slit the throats of the wives and children of the 800 men crucified before their eyes in a final, sadistic twist.

SLOWER OR MORE PAINFUL DEATH

The origins of this appalling way of killing are unclear, but its advocates included the Phoenicians, Greeks, Egyptians, Persians, and latterly the Romans. At first the methodology was simple: Victims were strapped to a single stake firmly rooted in the ground and left to die from thirst, starvation, or attack by wild animals. Crossbeams were introduced and the crucifix had either four points, like the Christian cross, three-points, as in a large letter T, or was X-shaped—known as the St. Andrew's cross, as he is believed to have died on such a construction.

Scripture bears out other historical evidence of the procedure in Roman times. The condemned were whipped and dragged the beam of the cross to the execution site (an entire cross would be too heavy for one man to move). At the cross the victim was nailed through the palms and feet, and wore only a loin cloth. The feet rested on a small wooden platform to help keep them in place. The judge sometimes showed pity and had crucified men killed before sundown. Death came more quickly, and more painfully, when legs or

BELOW: St. Andrew, one of the 12 apostles, wanted to be crucified on an X-shaped cross since he did not deem himself worthy to die in the same way as Jesus.

arms were broken. Nevertheless, the crucified often spent hours alive on the cross in the hot sun, at the mercy of hordes of insects.

In later years the cross was inverted, its top buried in the ground. Victims hung upside-down were hastened toward coma and death. Japanese crucifixions had further embellishments, with the executioner causing painful injuries without bringing the hour of death closer.

Constantine, the Roman emperor and convert to Christianity, abolished crucifixion in AD 337 as a mark of respect for Jesus. It was used in France until the 12th century and exists as a punitive option under the Islamic code today.

ABOVE: Albrecht Dürer uncompromisingly portrays Jesus being prepared for his crucifixion at Calvary in "The Nailing of Christ to the Cross," 1496. Although the cross was a commonplace Roman device for executions, it rapidly became adopted as the symbol of the Christian Church.

ROMAN TORTURE

The Romans regarded torture as a legitimate way of obtaining the truth in legal proceedings. The law permitted slaves and foreigners to be tortured before a specifically licensed court, and later it was commonplace in any case involving treason or sorcery.

RIGHT: Gladiatorial combat was the sport of choice for thousands of Roman citizens. This mosaic scene is at a Roman villa at Nennig in Germany's Saarland.

BELOW: A version of the rack is used to torture prisoners captured in Gaul. Other designs used heavy weights to stretch the limbs.

The decadence of the late Roman Empire and the absolute power invested in its rulers allowed the likes of Nero, Tiberius, and Caligula to pursue their sadistic inclinations unchecked. For these monsters, torture was almost a hobby.

Torture was a penalty in itself or a prelude to death or banishment. It was used for both civil and criminal offenses (creditors, for instance, were allowed to torture their debtors), and later, Christian emperors decreed heresy was punishable by flogging. The Roman flogging whip, or *flagellum*, would often kill.

The Roman historian Suetonius, writing in his *Lives of the Twelve Caesars*, described how Tiberius invented a method of torture to inflict on suspected lawbreakers. The emperor would force "the poor wretches to drink a great quantity of wine, and presently to tie their members with a lute string, that he might rack them at once with the girding of the string, and with the pressure of urine."

The rack, more properly known as the *equuleus* (young horse), was a favored instrument of torture and probably looked something like a gymnasium vaulting horse. It was equipped with heavy weights that were hung from the victim's limbs, slowly stretching him to death.

SAWING A MAN IN HALF

Tiberius was particularly sensitive to rumors of treason. When in AD 31 the commander of his Praetorian Guard, Lucius Aelius Sejanus, was suspected of murdering the emperor's only son, Drusus, a ruthless witch-hunt followed. Tiberius executed Sejanus and tortured almost everyone he thought he should mistrust. It was even claimed that he racked to death a close friend who merely happened to call on a social visit.

Tiberius's successor, Caligula, had a reputation for watching prisoners suffer while he ate. His torturers were told a victim should "feel himself die"—a term which required them to inflict dozens of small cuts and stab wounds to ensure a lingering end.

Caligula's many atrocities included sawing men in half and burning them alive as a sideshow in the Roman circus. According to Suetonius he once ordered a gladiator master to be "cramped with irons, and beaten for two days" and "did not kill him outright till his brain was putrefied and offended him with the stench."

Persecution of Christians (see page 14) was a feature of the late empire; the 4th century emperor Maximinus pursued this policy with particular relish. A description of the execution of Apphianus by the theologian Eusebius records how the prisoner was hung up high to suffer sharp combs being dragged down every side of his body. "His feet were burning in a sharp fire so that the flesh of his feet, as it was consumed, dropped like melted wax and the fire burst into his very bones like dry reeds."

THE GLADIATORS

Gladiatorial contests began in Rome in 264 BC, when three pairs fought at a funeral. By Trajan's victory celebrations in AD 107 the gladiator spectacle had developed into a massive industry, with 5000 pairs compelled to entertain the masses. Their greatest stage was undoubtedly the Colosseum in Rome, which could hold around 50,000 spectators. The desperate and often mismatched warriors were mainly drawn from the ranks of slaves, prisoners of war, and condemned criminals, though inevitably Christians were included.

THE FIRST MILLENNIUM

T he use of execution in religious ritual is older than any written history. It appears in almost every ancient culture and society, to varying degrees, and seems to revolve around three basic tenets: Firstly, that sacrificing human life appeases the gods. Secondly, wives or slaves of a deceased leader may be needed by him in the after-life—and must therefore die themselves and be buried with him—and lastly, the dead can help to protect the living.

This chapter looks at traditions of sacrifice throughout the first millennium and the elaborate rituals that accompanied them. Even for relatively unsophisticated cultures, such as those inhabiting northern Europe 2,000 years ago, the treatment of the condemned required preparation. Studies of the mysterious "bog bodies"—preserved corpses recovered from once-sacred peat bogs—show that in some cases their heads were partially shaved, and some archeologists suspect that the porridge they consumed as a last meal may have been ritually significant.

As cultures developed, so did the methods of sacrifice. The pagan Vikings would hang human offerings in sacred groves, convinced that putrefying flesh imbued the trees with spiritual power. Rus communities on the Volga adopted a centuries-old sacrificial ceremony in which a condemned female slave indulged in a series of sexual liaisons before her appointment with the strangulation cord of the "angel of death." The Druids, perhaps western Europe's most enigmatic sect, supposedly roasted human sacrifices *en masse* in huge wicker cages.

However, lack of written records makes it difficult to be certain about the death penalties of Europe's Dark Ages. More was recorded in China, and details of traditional punishments were greedily regurgitated by Western travelers in the 17th and 18th centuries, offering a treasure trove of shocking material for later fiction writers. Of many infamous techniques, the most fiendish was the "death of a thousand cuts," in which parts of the victim were gradually sliced away. Similar traditional punishments of the first millennium were still used hundreds of years later.

RIGHT: A gory and dramatic illustration of a Druidic ceremonial sacrifice. Many first millennium peoples performed such rituals, believing they would benefit the living. The essence of this Gallic scene is accurate, although there is considerable artistic licence.

THE VIKINGS: A HEATHEN DEATH

ABOVE: This 12th century tapestry shows Odin on the left, with thunder god Thor and fertility god Frey on the right.

RIGHT: Vikings disembark on the British coast.

SLAVES TO THE PYRE

The practice of killing slaves to accompany their masters into the spirit world is found in many early civilizations. Viking culture is no exception and something of the ritual involved can be seen from the writings of Ibn Fadlan during his stint in AD 921–2 as an ambassador from the King of Baghdad to the Bulgars on the River Volga. Ibn Fadlan tells how the female slave of a rich man would volunteer to die. She would spend her last days drinking, feasting, and having sex with his friends. Later they restrained her in the funeral boat, strangling her with cord, as an elderly woman called the Angel of Death plunged a dagger into the slave's chest. The boat and body would then be burned.

The Vikings had a sophisticated court system to deal out just punishment to their criminals. Their slaves weren't so lucky.

To understand Viking attitudes to crime and punishment is to negotiate a literary minefield of their epic poems and later histories written by Christian authors. The Vikings' runic alphabet was not suited to lengthy text and much of their law was spoken; the danger is in relying too heavily on the writings of 13th and 14th century historians who may have had their own agendas. We can make informed guesses about Viking methods from their sagas and the Danelaw that operated across much of northern England after the Norse invasion. Viking courts were known as "Things." They operated in public and it was the prerogative of all freeborn men to consult them over civil and criminal matters. There were laws on boundary rights (hunting and tree-felling), social behavior (satire, libel, writing love songs), petty criminality (turning a neighbor's butter sour or stealing his bees), and laws against rape and murder.

Things had a complex system of penalties, ranging from fines and banishment to the amputation of fingers, toes and limbs and, ultimately, execution. Hanging and beheading were both recognized forms of the death penalty but the way these sentences were enforced is less clear. Viking law depended heavily on the goodwill and co-operation of all parties, but it was often up to a litigant and his backers to carry out sentence.

GOD OF THE GALLOWS

Foreigners, and particularly Viking slaves, were in a much more vulnerable position. They had no legal rights and could be beaten, sexually abused, or killed on a whim by their owners. Masters who treated slaves badly were met with disapproval, in the same way a farmer might be criticized for poor stock-keeping, but slaves' lives were usually measured in cows, marks, or silver (8.5 ounces under Icelandic law).

It naturally followed that slaves were the automatic choice for ritual human sacrifice. Votive offerings to popular deities such as Odin (king and "god of the gallows"), Thor (thunder), and Frey (fertility) were made during pagan festivals, usually by hanging or drowning. In Book IV of *Gesta Hammaburgensis*, Adam of Bremen writes of a nine-yearly festival at a golden temple near Uppsala, Sweden that everyone was expected to attend with their sacrifices. Even converted Christians joined in.

"The bodies they hang in the sacred grove that adjoins the temple. Now the grove is so sacred in the eyes of the heathen that each and every tree in it is believed divine because of the death or putrefaction of the victims. Even dogs and horses hang there with the men, and a Christian told me that he had seen 72 bodies suspended promiscuously."

THE DRUIDS

ABOVE: The horrific wickerman, supposedly constructed by Druids and crammed with sacrificial humans, usually criminals sentenced to death.

There is something uniquely repulsive about the methods of execution allegedly employed by the Druids, the secretive religious and scholarly class of the European Celts. They devised the infamous wickerman.

The Druids wielded immense power—even over the kings in nominal control of Celtish tribes—and were universally feared. For a thousand years either side of the birth of Christ they defined themselves as the guardians of law and nature, using divination, ritual, and sacrifice to cement their social standing.

Of all the methods of punishment credited to the Druids, the most notorious is the "wickerman." These giant wood and straw cages made in the shape of men were filled with people and animals before being set alight.

According to Julius Caesar, writing about Gaul in 44 BC, the priests preferred to use criminals as convenient sacrificial victims, but if none could be found innocent people would be consecrated for the job. In his *De Bello Gallico* Caesar wrote:

"All the people of Gaul are completely devoted to religion, and for this reason those who are greatly affected by diseases and in the dangers of battle either sacrifice human victims or vow to do so using the Druids as administrators to these sacrifices, since it is judged that unless for a man's life a man's life is given back, the will of the immortal gods cannot be placated. In public affairs they have instituted the same kind of sacrifice. Others have effigies of great size interwoven with twigs, the limbs of which are filled up with living people which are set on fire from below, and the people are deprived of life surrounded by flames."

PROPAGANDA OR FACT?

Another classical author, Strabo, wrote in his *Geography* that the Celts would impale people in their temples and "strike a man who had been consecrated for sacrifice in the back with a sword, and make prophecies based on his death-spasms; and they would not sacrifice without the presence of the Druids."

There is little doubt that it was in Roman interests to demonize the Druids. Caesar needed to boost political support for his military campaigns in Gaul and what better way to manipulate opinion than to recount the bloodthirsty activities of Celtic tribes threatening the borders of the empire? The historian Cornelius Tacitus's account of the Roman attack on Anglesey, a Druid stronghold in North Wales, was in keeping with this stance. He reported altars "soaked with human blood"—but one wonders how he could be so sure, since animal sacrifices were almost certainly more common in Druid rituals.

The fact that these classical accounts should be treated with skepticism is not to suggest that the Druids were victims of propaganda. Wickerman executions are included in Celtic myths. The Welsh *Mabinogi*, for instance, refers to men being herded into wooden prisons specially constructed for incineration, and the Celtic deity Taranis was said to have been appeased by the burning of sacrifices.

Even more persuasive is the archeological record. Apart from the "bog bodies" (see page 32) there is evidence of dedicatory sacrifices, in which living people, particularly children, were interred in the foundations of new buildings. Traces of

human blood and flesh were found on a pole at the bottom of a late-Iron Age shaft at Holzhausen, Bavaria apparently for impaling victims. One of the most sickening examples of this mode of death was found at Garton Slack, Yorkshire, England, where a man and pregnant woman were found huddled together in a pit, their arms pinned together by a stake.

ABOVE: This melodramatic Victorian interpretation of Druidic sacrifice is titled "The Victim."

THE ANGLO-SAXONS

With no written records, we can only speculate about the lives of Anglo-Saxons. Were unusual burials a form of execution or an innocent custom?

By any measure, it was a terrible way to die. The woman was thrown on top of a coffin and apparently held down by her executioners as a heavy stone was placed on the small of her back. She was buried alive. Archeologists found her skeleton with leg bones kicked back and elbows raised, as though trying to push herself upward. Her fists were clenched in a hopeless attempt to scrabble free.

Found in an Anglo-Saxon cemetery at Sewerby, East Yorkshire this grave remains one of the most extraordinary archeological legacies from Britain in the Dark Ages. Some historians have speculated that she committed some heinous crime against the woman lying in the coffin below, possibly murder, and that the face-down position of the body is significant.

BELOW: The Vikings and Anglo-Saxons had legal systems. Here a tied prisoner is arraigned before his accuser at the Shire Moot, an early version of the English county court.

In the majority of known post-Roman burials the corpse is laid out straight on its back. There are some rarer instances of crouched and side-on interments, such as those at Cirencester, Ilchester, and Cannington, England but it is difficult to gauge whether these were down to local custom or had special significance.

As Anglo-Saxon culture spread across Britain it appears that face-down burials—notably at Poundbury, Ilchester, Lankhills, Radley, and Cirencester—began to emerge. The graves seem relatively well-furnished with possessions needed for the afterlife. They were not dug on the edges of burial grounds—a location that might have suggested the dead were outcasts.

One possibility is that face-down corpses were sacrifices, perhaps to provide spiritual servants for a dead nobleman or leader. Was the Sewerby woman buried in this way to ensure that she would become a slave in the next world?

A SHIP'S BURIAL

Evidence suggests human sacrifice was a part of early Anglo-Saxon Britain. At Lankhills, for instance, three decapitated skeletons were located near graves which were either very rich (in terms of grave goods) or ritually unusual. At Poundbury, a concentration of three decapitated bodies was found well to the west of the main cemetery area. Whether these people were outcasts, sacrificial victims, or executed criminals remains open to debate.

Rather more conclusive is the evidence from Sutton Hoo, that richly furnished, enigmatic cemetery in Suffolk that demolished the once-common view that early Anglo-Saxon culture was primitive. A seventh century ship was buried there, remarkable both for what it contained (beautifully worked weapons and jewelry) and what it did not (the remains of a corpse).

Academic and forensic scientists suspect that this amazing tomb once housed a body, perhaps that of a king, which over the years dissolved into the cemetery's acidic sand. The discovery of three decapitated bodies nearby was most intriguing. Decapitation can sometimes be explained as a way of freeing the body's spirit after death. In this case, however, the bodies were found with their hands tied behind their backs, which surely indicates they were executed.

The perennial problem for archeologists trying to understand religious belief and justice in the Dark Ages lies in the sheer diversity and mingling of cultures. The Anglo-Saxons arriving from Northern Europe may have brought their own set of values but the population would also have embraced Celtic and Roman laws, both of which may have been influenced by native customs. The big picture of a moral code in Europe only begins to emerge after the arrival of Christianity and a return to written records.

ABOVE: This ornately carved silver and gold Anglo-Saxon helmet was recovered from the site of the Sutton Hoo burial boat.

THE BOG BODIES

Of the hundreds of bog bodies recovered, some give remarkable insight into the victims' prehistoric lifestyle. But we cannot be sure whether they were murdered or sacrificed, or why.

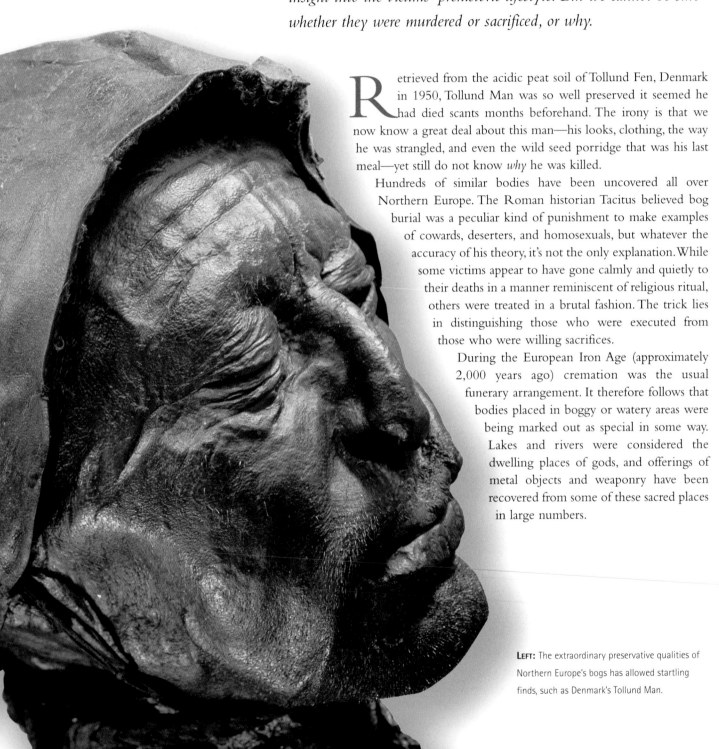

Retrieved from the acidic peat soil of Tollund Fen, Denmark in 1950, Tollund Man was so well preserved it seemed he had died scants months beforehand. The irony is that we now know a great deal about this man—his looks, clothing, the way he was strangled, and even the wild seed porridge that was his last meal—yet still do not know *why* he was killed.

Hundreds of similar bodies have been uncovered all over Northern Europe. The Roman historian Tacitus believed bog burial was a peculiar kind of punishment to make examples of cowards, deserters, and homosexuals, but whatever the accuracy of his theory, it's not the only explanation. While some victims appear to have gone calmly and quietly to their deaths in a manner reminiscent of religious ritual, others were treated in a brutal fashion. The trick lies in distinguishing those who were executed from those who were willing sacrifices.

During the European Iron Age (approximately 2,000 years ago) cremation was the usual funerary arrangement. It therefore follows that bodies placed in boggy or watery areas were being marked out as special in some way. Lakes and rivers were considered the dwelling places of gods, and offerings of metal objects and weaponry have been recovered from some of these sacred places in large numbers.

LEFT: The extraordinary preservative qualities of Northern Europe's bogs has allowed startling finds, such as Denmark's Tollund Man.

TOP RIGHT: While some bog bodies may have been sacrificial victims, there is no doubt that Lindow Man was savagely executed.

One of the most outstanding finds is the Gundestrup Cauldron, a highly ornate silver bowl probably fashioned around 200 BC in southeast Europe. The cauldron has 13 panels, each decorated with a Celtic deity encircled by mythological animals and various scenes of sacrifice. It had been deliberately buried in the bog at Gundestrup, Denmark close to the bodies of two women and a man, but how it arrived in the area and why such a valuable possession was cast away will never be known.

Among the more violent bog body deaths was that inflicted on Denmark's Huldremose Woman (c.AD 100). She was hacked with swords and had her right arm completely severed. The Grauballe Man (also Denmark, c. AD 310) died with his throat slit ear-to-ear, while Lindow Man (Cheshire, England c.AD 200) had been clubbed on the head, garotted, and wounded in the throat. Other victims were probably drowned, held underwater by executioners wielding forked sticks.

The fact that women and even adolescent girls were sent to the bogs strongly suggests a sacrificial element. The 14-year-old Windeby Girl (northern Germany, AD 1) had been blindfolded, with the left side of her head closely cropped before she was killed. The Yde Girl (Holland, c.AD 1) also had her head partially shaved but died a much more violent death by strangulation, perhaps indicating she was a criminal.

RITUAL OF HONOR?

A significant number of bog burials involved people of a wealthy or noble class, as evident from the lack of calluses on their hands. Some archeologists think it may have been a great honor to be selected for bog burial, arguing that this would explain the calm and peaceful demeanor of many victims. Tollund Man seems to support the theory because, despite the presence of the severed noose around his neck, his facial muscles were relaxed, his eyes closed and lips pursed; almost as though he spent his last moments meditating. It may even be that the porridge he ate was part of a death ritual. Traces of similar meals have been recovered from the guts of other victims.

THE END OF THE MILLENNIUM

Although cultures grew and developed, old methods of punishment remained. Barbaric tortures that originated in the first millennium continued into the next, to medieval times and even beyond.

"With superhuman command of self, the unhappy Mowung bore silently the slow and deliberate slicing-off—first of his cheeks, then of his breasts, the muscles of upper and lower arms, the calves of his legs, etc, care being taken throughout to avoid touching any immediately vital part." This "execution of twenty-one cuts" took place in the Japan of the Middle Ages; a closed society for centuries on end, its forms of torture and execution remained in use for generations.

Japan was not the only country in which brutal, archaic punishments outlived the first millennium by centuries. In 1813 in Syria—then part of the Ottoman Empire—surgeon Charles Lewis Meryon reported a death by impalement. The pole was forced up the body by means of a wooden mallet and the victim still alive when the pole was fixed upright "in a rude manner, for the Turks preserve no decorum in executions." The victim was put out of his misery with a bullet an hour later.

There is evidence of burying alive in the reign of Ivan the Terrible in Russia between 1547 and 1584, and in India under the reign of the Great Mogul Jahangir in 1618. We can be sure this crude form of execution originated in an early era.

In Russia it was the penalty for women who killed their husbands. Their heads were left above ground so they expired from exposure or thirst, but mercy was shown if the husbands were known to be violent. In such cases the woman was dispatched to a convent where they were fitted with chains and kept in solitary confinement until death.

SACRIFICED FOR THE SUN

The cruelty of the Great Mogul was inspired after he caught one of his wives kissing a eunuch. Since she was beyond the age of 30, the wife was no longer sexually active with the Mogul, but nevertheless she was buried up to her neck. Her head bared to the hot sun and her wails heard for a day-and-a-half. A British man reported: "[The] horrid execution, or rather murder, was acted near our house; where the eunuch, by the command of the said King was brought very near the place where this poor creature was thus buried alive, and there in his sight cut all to pieces."

BELOW: The Hindu tradition of Suttee, in which a wife "volunteers" to die on her deceased husband's funeral pyre, was outlawed in India in 1829.

Suttee, the self-sacrifice of wives upon their husbands' funeral pyres, has been in existence as part of Hindu tradition for centuries. It wasn't officially abolished in India until 1829.

Sacrifice was an integral part of the Mexican and South American cultures discovered by the Spanish in the 15th century but dating from centuries before. Conquistador Bernal Diaz de Castillo was a boy when he first visited one of Mexico's offshore islands, where he saw pyramid altars upon which five Indians had been sacrificed. "Their chests had been cut open and their arms and thighs had been cut off and the walls were covered with blood."

Later the Spaniards discovered that the severed limbs were ritually eaten in a sauce made of blood. Cannibalism was widespread and it is thought that the Aztecs deliberately fattened up slaves for the table. In 1487 20,000 victims were sacrificed at the dedication of the great temple Tenochtitlan, in the traditional belief that the sun had to be fed with blood to prevent its destruction.

ABOVE: Spanish conquistadors who plundered Aztec treasure could expect a dreadful death if caught by its owners. The usual form of sacrifice involved cutting out the victim's beating heart.

BEFORE THE AGE OF REASON

By the Middle Ages, the innovations in torture and execution in Europe were no longer base, instinctive ways to harm and kill but were conceived to increase the suffering of the victim.

Capital crimes of the era included murder, of course, but also poaching, stealing fruit from trees, damaging orchards, forgery, and debt. Ahead in the league of punishments was hanging. In England the other favored option was branding; the trend was toward immediate punishments rather than anything that took time. Only a few people were imprisoned.

There would finally come an era where juries refused to convict if they knew the offender would hang for a trivial offense. Some people even refused to prosecute. Accordingly, secular law would ultimately be undermined—although not before numerous poor souls had been sacrificed as public examples.

Ecclesiastical law was a different matter. The Church wielded enormous power in the Middle Ages and did everything in its power to keep that position secure. The Pope and his cardinals suffered from paranoia in much the same way as 20th century dictators, who chose to eliminate rivals rather than intellectually defend their positions. This was a time of faith inspired by fear, God's retribution in Heaven, and the harsh justice the Church imposed upon those who opposed it on Earth.

RIGHT: The array of punishments in medieval times was great and applied to a staggering array of misdemeanors. Each one meant mighty suffering for the victim, but in some cases their suffering was a form of amusement. The spectacle of execution attracted crowds of black-humored folk, and when criminals were restrained in devices like stocks people applied punishment by throwing objects.

AX AND BLOCK

While the executioner's ax was hefty, its cutting edge was rarely sharpened. It killed not by a clean cut but mostly by crushing. Several blows were often necessary to part the head from the body.

A GRIM DISPLAY

Severed heads could further be used as part of a grim propaganda program by the king of the day. They were boiled in salt and displayed on spikes—in London usually on London Bridge, for years the only point where the River Thames could be crossed. The heads might stay there for months. This backfired when John Fisher was executed in King Henry VIII's war against the Pope in 1535. As witness Dr. Thomas Baily testified, "it grew daily fresher and fresher, so that in his lifetime he never looked so well… many people took [it] to be miracle that Almighty God had showed the innocence and holiness of this blessed father." The order came for the head to be tossed into the Thames.

Victims of the ax were first paraded to the scene of their death. The more notorious the candidate, the higher the scaffold to afford the largest crowds a view. Before the condemned was a stout block of oak to cradle their neck. With a blindfold in place, the victim was helped into position, prostrate before the executioner. A high block was provided for most noblemen and women; a low block further compounded the indignity of death.

It was customary for the executioner to brandish the severed head of those judged to be enemies of the state with the words: "Behold the head of a traitor! So die all traitors!"

RIGHT: The condemned person knelt before a roughly hewn block of oak, laid their neck across it, and steadied themselves. The ax was usually blunt and its user unskilled.

Still, the high-born of Britain preferred to be dispatched in this manner—indeed, they were not above begging a judge for the ax. As late as 1760, the 4th Earl Ferrers, guilty of murdering a steward, was horrified at the thought of being hanged. When his protestations to the judge failed, he asked for a silk rope. Ferrers went to his death at Tyburn, like other common criminals.

Not all those on the scaffold co-operated. Margaret, Countess of Salisbury, was the mother of one of the cardinals who vociferously opposed King Henry VIII—who sentenced the entire family to death. On May 27, 1541 she was led out to Tower Green, in the grounds of the Tower of London, where she refused to lie with her head on the block, declaring it was for traitors "and I am none." The executioner had to pursue her around the platform, swinging wildly.

INCOMPETENT AXMAN

Convicted of plotting against King Charles II in 1683, Lord Russell laid his head on the block. He handed executioner Jack Ketch a purse of money, a traditional gesture among the nobility. But Ketch's first blow missed entirely. "You dog, did I give you ten guineas to use me so inhumanely?" Lord Russell rebuked. Ketch took numerous blows to sever the head.

A fellow conspirator, Lord Monmouth, suffered the same horrors two years later, with Ketch wielding three blows and leaving the job unfinished. He flung down his ax, claiming "my heart fails me." The crowd called for Ketch's own death. He finished the grim task with a knife.

The last man to die by the ax in Britain was 80-year-old Lord Lovat, one of the leaders of the 1745 Jacobite rebellion, on April 8, 1747 at Tower Hill. So great was the crowd of onlookers that a specially constructed grandstand collapsed, killing 22 people. Executioner John Thrift thankfully accomplished his task with one blow.

VICTIMS

To some he was a tyrannical and two-faced monarch; to others he was respected and even revered as a ruler during troubled times. History is divided in its opinion of the controversial King Charles I, but he earned the admiration of many for the dignified manner in which he met his death.

England had been divided by civil war. The army decided the country could unite only with the death of the king. On January 20, 1649 he was charged before Parliament with high treason "against the realm of England," although the king did not plead, refusing to recognize the newly streamlined House of Commons as a court of law. A week later he was sentenced to death.

He requested warm clothing: "The season is so sharp as probably may make me shake, which some observers may imagine proceeds from fear. I would have no such imputation."

On January 30 Charles marched from St. James' Palace to the scaffold outside the Banqueting House in Whitehall, London to the ominous sound of beating drums. He mounted the scaffold to make a quiet speech, stating his sincere beliefs that the people should have no stake in government. "A subject and a sovereign are clean different things," he declared, describing himself as "the martyr of the people." "I go from a corruptible to an incorruptible Crown, where no disturbance can be."

Then he prepared himself for death. He tucked his cavalier curls into a white satin cap, to better reveal his neck. Charles told the executioner to wait for the signal—the outstretching of his arms—before wielding the blade, but the impatient axman almost acted too soon. After urging the executioner to wait for the sign, Charles completed his prayers. He slowly spread his arms and the ax quickly fell.

TRYING THE BLOCK OF SIZE

Fearing retribution from royalists, the executioners wore false beards and padded costumes, but it is certain that the slayers were Richard Brandon—"Young Gregory," as he was popularly known—and assistant William Lowen. Brandon, who received £30 and the king's handkerchief as payment, died within six months. Many believe he was grief-stricken at taking Charles I's life.

Much noble blood was spilled on the block. Perhaps the most tragic deaths were those of the women. Marriage to King Henry VIII had already proved to be a treacherous business. Catherine Howard saw her cousin Anne Boleyn put to death for

arousing the king's displeasure. She still risked marriage to him in 1540—and within two years was facing the same fate. Howard too was accused of infidelity. Her screams for mercy as she was dragged away by guards are still said to ring around the corridors of Hampton Court Palace in the dead of night.

Howard regained her composure, however: On the eve of the execution she had the ax's block brought to her cell and knelt before it. Satisfied that the block was the correct size, Howard was beheaded on February 15, 1542, on the same day as lady-in-waiting Lady Rochford, whose husband had been executed at Henry's bidding.

Lady Jane Grey was the victim of family politics. Her family pitted her as Queen against rightful heir Mary I in 1553. Compelled to abdicate, she was convicted of treason and beheaded at the Tower of London—after seeing the coffin of husband Lord Guildford Dudley carted past her chamber window.

Mary, Queen of Scots was calm in the face of her executioners at Fotheringhay Castle. It took three blows to end her life.

SWORDSMEN

When Anne Boleyn was sentenced to death for high treason against her husband, King Henry VIII, she carefully considered her options. In the end she opted for the continental choice, that of swordsman.

For those that gathered around the five-foot scaffold built on Tower Green on May 19, 1536, it was a rare glimpse at European punishment. As there was no one in England who knew the job, a swordsman was bought over from Calais—still in England's possession at the time. He was dressed in a tight black suit and a high, horn-shaped cap, his features made more monstrous by a sinister half-mask.

His weapon, a hefty sword, was hidden beneath the straw that covered the scaffold until the doomed queen finished her prayers. The single strike that removed Anne's head was so sudden that her lips and eyes were fluttering even as he held it aloft. The day's work cost the Exchequer 100 crowns.

It may have been one of history's great miscarriages of justice. Anne was imprisoned at the Tower of London just 17 days before her death, accused of incest with her brother, adultery with four others, and conspiracy to kill the king.

Henry VIII had spent a great deal of effort ridding himself of his first wife, Catherine of Aragon, a move that brought him into direct conflict with the Catholic church. He had no intention of repeating the costly episode.

Anne was pregnant when they wed in 1533 and Henry wanted a male heir. But a girl, the future Elizabeth I, was born. The king claimed that the six-fingered queen bewitched him, and he turned his attentions to Jane Seymour, his future wife. Anne may or may not have committed adultery; she certainly fell victim to Henry's increasingly irrational behavior.

DYING BY THE SWORD

The sword was well used in both Germany and France (until the arrival of the guillotine). Beheading by sword appears to have been imported from France at least once by William the Conqueror, who ordered the death of a troublesome earl by this means in 1076.

In general the swords were long, weighty, with a blunt or rounded blade measuring some two inches wide. It provided a cleaner cut than the ax but its administration required considerable skill. As there was no block to steady the victim, he or she was required to kneel and calmly bare their neck. If they flinched in terror, the sword might slice into their head or shoulder. Weak victims were occasionally permitted to sit in a chair.

The skill of French executioner Charles-Henri Sanson was such that he could kill with a single blow. Chevlier de la Barre was condemned for refusing to salute some monks. He didn't consider himself a criminal and refused to kneel. Sanson wielded the sword in a flash, leaving the body upright with the severed head sitting on the shoulders.

Traditionally, the baying crowds loathed executioners, but one in Germany was warmly applauded for beheading two men at once. Not all victims were so lucky. In 1626 it took 29 blows to decapitate Comte de Chalais.

The sword was favored in Japan. A graveyard recently excavated in Tokyo was found to contain 105 skulls, apparently severed by samurai sword. Experts believe that as many as 200,000 people met their swift end here, one of two execution sites in the city. While beheading by sword was fazed out in Europe by the end of the 18th century, it occurred in Japan for at least another hundred years.

ABOVE: Anne Boleyn was just one of Henry VIII's victims, but her method of execution was unique in England.

LEFT: With their target kneeling unrestrained and shaking with fear, swordsmen required great skill to accurately make the killing stroke.

THE BLOODY CODES

The excesses of the guillotine during the French Revolution are well publicized. Yet the gallows in England were likewise responsible for numerous unjust deaths.

ABOVE: This crumbling parchment illustrates the agony and ignominy of hanging in medieval times.

Hanging was the favored method of executing murderers by medieval English law. However, in 1723 the Waltham Black Act made a broad spectrum of other offenses punishable by death, including forgery, bestiality, burning a haystack, and appearing at a roadside with a sooty face!

The numbers taking a final walk to the scaffold escalated out of all proportion. While there were 281 hangings in London during the first half of the 18th century, numbers exceeded 1,200 in the second half—and the number continued to escalate nationwide in the 19th century.

Trials were swift, with minimum representation for the illiterate. Juries were prejudiced against the lower social orders and most judges were inclined toward the death penalty.

There was a somewhat random appeals process. This took about six weeks and, during that time, convicts were seen to age prematurely, with black hair turning gray and smooth faces becoming lined. Although the rate of pardons ultimately increased from approximately 50 to 90 percent to keep pace with convictions during crime waves, the number of people sent to hang for non-violent crimes remained colossal.

In early times hanging was an unsophisticated business, carried out with a rope slung over the branch of a tree. Later the tree was replaced by a wooden gallows, with the condemned forced to climb a ladder to meet the noose. When the rope was secured they were "turned off" the ladder, to slowly choke. Highwayman Dick Turpin died in this way at York, launching himself off the ladder into death.

RIDING TOWARD DEATH

In later years, the condemned traveled by cart, with their back to the scaffold, the rope around their necks, arms bound behind them and sitting on their coffin. Sometimes they were dressed in shrouds. Arriving under the crossbeam of the gallows, the hangman tied the rope to the scaffold before driving the horses on, leaving the victim dangling helpless.

With the victims came the ordinaries, men of God who were determined to get confessions. Consequently, they provided little spiritual comfort in their attempt to tie up legal loose ends.

From 1752 the bodies of hanged men were awarded to surgeons who sought to push back the boundaries of medical knowledge by dissection. It was the final ignominy in an age that set great store in burial of the intact body.

NO GALLOWS FOR WOMEN

For women the punishment was not hanging but burning at the stake. Merciful executioners pulled a noose tight around their necks before they burned to death. In 1786, when Phoebe Harris was burned at a stake planted in the middle of Newgate Street, the site of the prison, 20,000 people gathered to watch. The burning of women was not abolished until 1790.

Hanging became ingrained in English culture but a creeping repugnance for it prompted by the Enlightenment forced political changes. In 1830, Sir Robert Peel said: "It is impossible to conceal from ourselves that capital punishments are more frequent and the criminal law more severe on the whole in this country than in any country in the world."

In 1837 the death sentence was repealed for petty crimes and the number of people destined to become "gallows' apples" plummeted. The nation was left in wonder at its long-term tolerance for the bloody codes.

ABOVE: This illustration from 1475 shows a man already in his shroud, dead in the noose. It betrays none of the suffering he underwent while he slowly strangled.

TRAFFIC AT TYBURN

Many British towns possessed gallows and celebrated pitiless hanging days, but none were as busy as Tyburn. A three-cornered crossbeam capable of hanging 24 people at a time—the "triple tree"—was used every six weeks.

Before they hanged at Tyburn, prisoners were held at Newgate Prison, where people flocked to gawk at the more notorious of the condemned. James Maclaine, dubbed "The Gentleman Highwayman" for the respect he displayed to his young female victims, received 3,000 visitors. People attended the Condemned Sermons in the prison chapel on the Sundays prior to executions, which were ticket-only events when infamous criminals were involved.

During the night before an execution, the bellman from St Sepulchre's Church nearby struck up a mournful tolling and read aloud: "All you that in the condemned hold do lie; Prepare you, for tomorrow you shall die. Watch all, and pray, the hour is drawing near; That you before the Almighty must appear. Examined well yourselves, in this time repent; That you may not to eternal flames be sent. And when St. Sepulchre's bells tomorrow tolls; The Lord have mercy on your souls." Merchant Taylor Robert Dove gave £50 in 1604 for this doleful verse to be read three times, in the hope that the doomed person would repent.

The journey from Newgate to Tyburn was some three miles and took several hours. The criminals were feted if they were popular and pelted with rotten fruit and vegetables if they were not. A guard of constables and civic dignitaries, such as the city marshal and sheriff, accompanied the prisoner's cart. It was customary to stop at an inn for some refreshment *en route*.

NO ESCAPE FROM TYBURN

Those killed at Tyburn number in the thousands and include highwayman Isaac Atkinson in 1640, who was 26. In his final speech Atkinson said, "Gentlemen, there's nothing like a merry life, and a short one." Rev. Robert Foulkes was hanged in 1679 for the murder of his mistress's newborn baby.

The proficient escape artist Jack Sheppard died at Tyburn on November 16, 1724, in front of 200,000 people. Five times he had defied fetters and cells from various secure accommodation in London. People gathered in anticipation of a further sensational escape, but none was forthcoming. Sheppard hanged for 15 minutes before a soldier cut him down. After the requisite attempts to resuscitate him failed, his body was borne away from the waiting anatomists to a respectable burial. A year later the thief taker Jonathan Wild was hanged half-conscious, having attempted suicide by poison. A prolific informer, his activities had sent many to the gallows.

John Franks, elderly and blind, was hanged on April 12, 1780 for stealing two damaged silver spoons from his former master—Jeremy Bentham, the famous reformer. The last person to be executed at Tyburn was John Austin, who died on November 7, 1783. By then London was large enough to encompass Tyburn and hanging days caused considerable chaos in the city. A replacement gallows was put up outside Newgate Prison.

ABOVE: Dick Turpin—depicted here in Cambridge holding up a fellow highwayman—was hanged in York at the age of 34. Although his death was premature, he lived in an era when few reached their 40s, claimed by the judicial system or disease.

LEFT: Executions at Tyburn attracted huge crowds. Given the body of constables in attendance, the likelihood of escape was slim.

PILGRIMAGE FOR THE MARTYRS

A Catholic pilgrimage to Tyburn to honor 105 martyrs was set to be axed after 2000 because it caused disruption in London's premier shops. Hundreds of pilgrims have followed the two-mile route of the doomed Catholics from the Old Bailey—the site of Newgate Prison—to Marble Arch every year since 1909. Following the march the pilgrims visited the Benedictine nunnery there, which keeps relics of the martyrs. Prayers were said for Catholic and Protestant martyrs of the 16th and 17th centuries.

A FESTIVAL OF DEATH

ABOVE: "Gin Lane," by William Hogarth (1697–1764), illustrates the evils of hard liquor. More than 9,000 children died from drinking gin in 1751.

Once, people flocked to hangings much the same as they crowd in to see baseball games today. If the victims were famous, the number of onlookers at these "Tyburn Fairs" swelled from approximately 5,000 to as many as 40,000, bubbling with banter and ale.

According to the writer Bernard Mandeville, the hanging days in England were "one continued fair, for whores and rogues of the meaner sort.... Apprentices and journeymen to the meanest trades are the most honorable part of these floating multitudes. All the rest are worse."

As a rule he was correct, although there's evidence that the politer classes attended when there was a sense of occasion about a hanging. If possible they hired a window with a vantage point to survey the scene. Even aristocrats had been known to join the judges as spectators. However, the snaggle-toothed women, leery men, and mischievous urchins arrayed before the scaffold were the final motley view beheld by the condemned.

FUN OF THE FAIR

There was plenty of entertainment while the mob waited for the victim to arrive. Gin sellers and bakers hawked their wares. The air rang with the voices of dramatists relating the crimes of the doomed. Some broke out into ballads about the victim, and a variety of bawdy songs were well known to the crowd. A couplet from verses that appeared in *Punch* magazine sums up the vulgar thrill felt by spectators. "Hurrah, you dogs, for hangin', the feelings to excite, I could ha' throttled Bill almost, that moment, with delight." In later years vividly illustrated pamphlets and sensationally worded newspapers were on sale, often authored by unscrupulous ordinaries. Pick-pockets were diligently at work, occasionally ensuring their own visit to the gallows.

People were responsive to the victim. They hoped to see a cheerful countenance, with proud bearing and unfailing courage in the face of death. It was called "dying game." This frequently occurred, with victims dancing on the scaffold, calling out to the crowd, and genially taking part in the festive atmosphere. Robert Hartley, hanged at Maidstone, Kent in 1823, gave a bow to the crowd and wished all a Happy New Year.

A STRANGE KINDNESS

Some bold victims indulged in gallows humor, instantly earning the respect of the mob. One highwayman allegedly sparred with the hangman over the tightness of the noose: "Hold, you rascal, have you a mind to strangle me?" Those who began rambling speeches in the hope of a last-minute reprieve were less popular. The crowd exhibited only limited patience before baying for action.

Many of the doomed wore elegant outfits, to exit in style. Highwaymen had a particular reputation for panache and courage in such circumstances.

However, there were those who failed to indulge the crowd in its desire for smiles and songs. Fear reduced many to clammy, trembling wrecks, incapable of weeping, talking, or even standing.

When the victim was left hanging it was not uncommon for them to urinate or defecate. The dying convulsed violently, spluttered, and sometimes bled from the ears. The crowd was often witness to goggling eyes, lolling tongues, and the other dreadful symptoms of slow strangulation, clearly visible when the victim refused to wear a hood.

An agonizing death usually gave the crowd no pleasure. At the urging of the mob, the hangman occasionally sped up the process by swinging on the victim's legs. Sometimes relatives did the same.

BELOW: Hogarth turned his attention to the crowds at Tyburn hangings. This graphic view is titled "Industry and Idleness."

HANGED, DRAWN AND QUARTERED

ABOVE: Fawkes and his accomplices failed to destroy the Houses of Parliament on November 5, 1605. The members of the Gunpowder Plot were hanged, drawn, and quartered.

The fate of criminals deemed so dire that mere death was not enough was barbarous. The process of hanging, drawing and quartering was as severe as executions became.

The sentence pronounced on the Duke of Buckingham in 1521 was horrifically detailed: "You shall be taken to the King's prison, the Tower of London, and there laid on a hurdle and so drawn to the place of execution, and there to be hanged and cut down alive; your members be cut off and cast into the fire; your bowels burnt before your eyes; your head smitten off and your body quartered and divided at the king's will. And God have mercy on your soul."

Such judgement was the dreadful consequence of treachery for men in England for more than five centuries (women were hanged and burnt). David, Prince of Wales, is thought to have been the first to face such appalling treatment, at Shrewsbury in 1283. Under Edward III the punishment was instituted more widely. Cratwell, an executioner during the reign of Henry VIII, was praised by the Lord Chancellor as "a conninge butcher in the quarteringe of men."

Although some victims were drawn to the scaffold by a horse, the "drawn" part of the punishment refers to the drawing of the intestines from their stomach. A small slit was made and the innards slowly and painfully extracted, and sometimes burned. If carefully done, the butchered person remained conscious throughout and death only came when the body was quartered with ax blows.

Guy Fawkes and other members of the Gunpowder Plot suffered the grim indignity after they were caught on November 5, 1605. Protestant followers of the Duke of Monmouth were similarly dealt with 80 years later, after an attempted uprising against James II. It was a black spot in British history, thanks largely to the callous judge Sir George Jeffreys. Traveling around the southwest, from where most of the rebels had been drawn, Jeffreys conducted the "Bloody Assizes" that ended in approximately 250 people being hung, drawn and quartered.

HANGED AND DECAPITATED

Following the Jacobite rebellion of 1745, Catholics again felt the wrath of law. Their punishment was further embellished, as their heads were spiked over Temple Bar gateway, London but the merciful executioner ensured they were dead before carving up their bodies.

But shockingly the sorry method of execution continued as late as 1820, albeit in a diluted form. Following the Cato Street Conspiracy that threatened to overthrow the government, eight condemned men were decapitated rather than quartered, and the executioners ensured the initial hanging killed them.

Commentators at the time believed a surgeon carried out the task. At last it was no longer felt necessary to cut out the traitor's heart for symbolic effect.

A crowd estimated at 100,000 gathered to see the Cato Street conspirators die outside Newgate Prison. The spectators included many from the higher orders of society who felt directly threatened by the plans of Arthur Thistlewood, the idealistic leader of the plotters.

Afterward, an overhaul in the system of punishments meant the ax was never raised again in such a manner. Although the mob was disapproving of the punishment, the executions caused little public condemnation or adverse newspaper comment.

Successive executioners were not moved by the horror of their tasks. They ensured there was plenty of sawdust on the scaffold to soak up the blood and kept a knife at hand in case the ax proved too blunt. If they fumbled it was because they were unfamiliar with the procedure, as beheadings became ever rarer.

THE GIBBET

When hangings failed to bring down the crime rate in 18th century England, the lawmakers developed another deterrent. The body of a hanged convict swung upon a gibbet near the scene of his crime, to strike horror into the hearts of passers-by.

Britain's Murder Act of 1752 permitted dead men to be hung by a chain as part of the sentence for serious misdemeanors. It could occur after or instead of dissection by surgeons. Sometimes the gibbet the corpse was suspended from was similar to a tall scaffold. Others were cages, which housed the corpses and preserved them against the ravages of nature or rescue attempts by concerned relatives. Bodies were often doused in tar to make them last longer.

A few people were hung in chains while still alive, left to die of thirst or exposure. Highwayman John Whitfield suffered such a fate near Carlisle in 1777. Unpopular for his crimes against local people, no rescue bids were forthcoming. Out of pity a coachman dispatched him with a bullet some days into the punishment.

Highwaymen were often gibbeted as a stark warning to others considering the same

BELOW: In Paris the gibbets at Montfaucon held ranks of corpses, creating a most affecting sight.

trade, so rural routes throughout the country were peppered with gibbets. Travelling alone at night and chancing upon the sight was morbidly frightening: "The chains rattled, the iron plates scarcely kept the gibbet together and the rags of the highwaymen displayed their horrible skeletons," wrote one observer. Poet William Wordsworth fled from an empty gibbet "faltering and faint." Many travelers took lengthy detours to miss these dreadful sights.

Yet urban gibbets became a popular Sunday afternoon destination for city folk, many of whom took their children along, assuming the fearful sight would act as a deterrent. Three bodies gibbeted at Wimbledon in 1795 apparently attracted a large proportion of London's population one summer's day.

THE REMAINS OF MORTALITY

Bodies remained on the gibbet for weeks or months, sometimes until the bones became weathered and brittle and collapsed. Friends and family tried to save loved ones from this final humiliation; accordingly the gibbet that held Adam Graham in 1747 was 36 feet high and studded with nails (his crime was not recorded). An unknown person set light to a gibbet in Derbyshire bearing the remains of three highwaymen. Given that the dead men were coated in tar, the flames were so intense that all was reduced to ashes.

In a letter to Home Secretary Robert Peel in 1824, William Sykes argued for the abolition of the gibbet at the Port of London, where the decomposing bodies of errant sailors and pirates were displayed. The "scarecrow remains of the poor wretches who long since expiated by death their crimes" were offensive to female travelers and an insult to sailors. "The remains of mortality is a sad sight under any circumstances, under such circumstances it is revolting, disgusting, pitiable, dishonorable to the law's omnipotence, and discreditable to the administrators of the law."

In 1832 the last two men to be gibbeted in England were hoisted aloft. They were miner William Jobling from the northeast coast and bookbinder George Cook of Leicestershire, both convicted of murder. The separate events attracted large, appreciative crowds.

But distaste for the practice in polite society made itself felt in government. During the parliamentary debate that led to its abolition in 1834, Lord Suffield asserted that the dire warning intended by the gibbet was lost on the populace. Its only effect, he said, "was that of scaring children and brutalizing the minds of the people. It could produce no moral effect whatever."

ABOVE: Suspended metal cages rattled in the wind. Birds and vermin stripped away the flesh but the body often remained in the rags it was hanged in.

BURNING

As a child, Queen Mary I was relegated from princess to little more than servant as a result of the political adventures of her father, Henry VIII. On her ascendancy to the throne, she used fire and Catholicism to exercise her ire.

Mary was disowned by Henry VIII and watched her mother, Catherine of Aragon, divorced and marginalized. Mary found herself in a loveless marriage put under intolerable strain when she underwent the charade of a phantom pregnancy. Throughout her troubles, Mary clung to Roman Catholicism for comfort. Even that was under duress, as Henry and his son Edward VI sought to impose Protestantism on England.

When Mary came to the throne in 1553 on the death of her half-brother, she was an embittered, hard-faced, and hard-line monarch determined to reverse the Reformation. Her favored means of doing so was burning at the stake.

Mary ruled for just five years until her death in November 1558. During her tenure nearly 300 people died in flames, all refusing to deny their Protestant faith. Excavations carried out three centuries afterward established that 43 died at London's Smithfield.

Among the most famous of Mary's martyrs were Nicholas Ridley and Hugh Latimer, who died together on 16 October 1555 before Balliol Hall, Oxford. As the pyre was lit, Latimer told his fellow bishop, "Be of good courage, Brother Ridley, and play the man; for we shall this day light such a candle by God's grace in England as I trust shall never be put out."

Later it was considered indecent for women to be hung, drawn, and quartered, so those found guilty of treason or murder went to the stake. To ease their suffering, the condemned were strangled before the bales around their feet were ignited.

BURNED FOR THEIR SUCCESS

As recently as 1777 a girl of 14 was to be burnt for a fiscal offense. A dignitary, Lord Weymouth, passed by chance and stopped the barbarous event. Death by burning was finally abolished in Britain in 1790.

England was not alone in its use of burning. It featured throughout Europe in the grisly pursuit of witches and heretics by the Catholic Church, and was notoriously employed to wipe out swathes of Jews during the 14th century.

The Black Death ravaged Europe in the mid-14th century, with an estimated death toll of 25 million. This

dreadful flea-borne disease had catastrophic consequences for the Jews, as wild rumors, first in Switzerland then in Germany, France, and England, insisted they were to blame. It was said that they poisoned wells in a bid to increase their wealth and power. Jewish people were arrested and tortured into confession. A few wise voices in the local authorities of church and council were drowned by the baying of the mob. Attempts to save the Jews were only successful in the domain of Avignon, where the Pope was then seated.

The burning at Strasbourg on St. Valentine's Day in 1349 was typical. About 2,000 Jews were herded onto a wooden platform built in the Jewish cemetery, where they were offered their freedom if they agreed to be baptized into the Christian Church. About half seized the chance to live. The rest were burned alive. Onlookers pulled children from the flames and baptized them against the will of their parents.

Debts owed to Jews were consequently canceled and the wealth of the dead was divided between the Church and feudal lords. Not for the last time, Jews were scapegoats for the terrible ills of society and penalized for their success in trade.

ABOVE: The Spanish Inquisition resulted in the death of thousands. The Inquisitors' targets were primarily Jews and heretics, although their prevailing greed left all merchants at risk.

TOP LEFT: Queen Mary I (1515–58) became known as Bloody Mary for her campaign against Protestants.

LEFT: John Badby died at Smithfield in 1410. He was convicted of heresy for casting doubt on the ritual of communion.

EXECUTION DEVICES IN MEDIEVAL EUROPE

Outside England, where hanging, burning, and decapitation were the favored means of execution, devices such as the mazzatello, garrote, and wheel were employed. They inflicted considerable pain before death came as a blessed release.

ABOVE: Spanish anarchists are publicly executed by garotte, their bodies steadied by seat, post, and restraints.

I n the eyes of the righteous, suffering was just as important as death in medieval Europe. Accordingly, criminals in France and German were broken on the wheel, an ancient form of execution presumably dating back almost as far as the invention of the wheel, some 2,000 years BC.

A large wheel was laid on a scaffold and the prisoner tied across it, his arms and legs attached to its outer rim. The executioner used an iron bar to attack the prisoner's limbs, breaking each in several places.

With the prisoner in agony, the wheel was propped up so observers could get a better view. Sometimes the injuries already sustained were sufficient to cause death. If the victim lingered for too long, the executioner wielded the bar against the chest several times.

Received wisdom says that St. Catherine of Alexandria was condemned to die on the wheel in the early years of the fourth century. Roman Emperor Maxentius sent philosophers to demolish her argument for Christianity, but she converted them. Legend says the wheel miraculously collapsed, as if it refused to support her death. Ultimately she was beheaded. Catherine became a popular martyr and gave her name to the Catherine Wheel firework. However, some doubt that she ever existed.

Rotating wheels were used in torture, too. A fire might be lit beneath and the wheel slowly turned so different parts of the body tied to the outer rim were burned. The wheel might be rolled through water or over a bed of nails.

A GLORIFIED STRANGULATION

In Spain the adopted method for capital punishment was the garrote. At first this was similar to hanging, but the victim kept both feet on the ground. The executioner simply strangled them using rope. However, there was room for improvement, and it duly arrived in the form of a post with a hole bored through it. Now the prisoner could stand or sit before the post, with the rope looped around his neck and threaded back through the post. Standing behind, the executioner pulled hard and death followed.

Later versions of the garrote had a stick on which the rope was twisted and consequently tightened. Then there was an iron collar with a screw that was gradually wound into the victim. Efficiency was increased when a small blade was attached to the garrote to sever the spinal cord.

In Catholic Spain the condemned observed a ritual that involved a night of prayer before the day of execution, in the company of two fire-and-brimstone clergymen. In the morning the prisoner was asked for a confession—executions could not go ahead without admission of guilt. Rather than face further torture or more hours in religious introspection, most readily confessed.

In Italy some victims were clubbed to death in front of crowds. In this gruesome method of execution, the prisoner stood with his back to the executioner. The masked killer brought down the *mazzatello*—or mallet—on the head of the victim, felling him with the mighty blow and probably shattering his skull. The executioner then set about the poor fellow with a knife, slitting his throat. Death by mazzatello was finally abolished after the Italian states were united under Garibaldi's leadership.

ABOVE: St. Catherine of Alexandria martyred on the wheel (painting by Tintoretto, c.1590). Recently scholars have begun to doubt that she ever existed.

WATER TORTURE

In medieval times God was perceived as an all-powerful presence who would protect His own. Accordingly, innocent men could expect divine intervention to prevent them from drowning when they were plunged into water.

ABOVE: Ducking stools were used to punish women. The rapid descent into cold water caused fatalities among older victims.

BELOW: Trial by water relied on the intervention of God to save the righteous.

Out of the firmly held belief in divine intervention came trial by ordeal. The "trial" began with religious ritual that lasted up to three days. The accused underwent prayer, fasting, exorcism, and other rites before attempting to prove his innocence.

With the preparation complete, a pot of water was boiled. The victim had to put a hand, or arm up to the elbow, into the scalding liquid. Three days later, guilt was discerned through the condition of the wound. If it appeared to be healing, the man had won God's blessing and was innocent. If it was open and sore, the man had been deserted in his hour of need and was guilty.

Other trials used cold water. The accused was bound by ankles and feet and lowered into a river or harbor with a rope tied around his waist. A knot was tied in the rope some distance from the body. If it was wet when the man was hauled up, he was innocent. If the water—broadly thought of as holy—had repelled the body and the knot was dry, he was guilty.

In trial by fire the accused walked across hot coals or carried lumps of heated iron. Once again, the injuries were inspected to ascertain guilt. Trial by combat assumed that God would defend the righteous. One man would pit his strength against another in a form of duel, with weaker specimens appointing a champion to fight their corner.

The results were not always in the hands of God. A bribe paid to those in charge could substantially reduce the temperature of the water or coals. When fixing became widespread, the Pope banned trial by ordeal in 1215.

BOILED TO DEATH

Although it was little used, the penalty of boiling to death existed in England and claimed at least two poor souls. In 1531 Richard Roose was convicted of poisoning 17 people in the Bishop of Rochester's house, killing two. To deter further skullduggery in the kitchen, a special law was made by which felons were boiled to death and banned from having the last rites. Before the statute was erased 16 years later, maid Margaret Dawe met the same fate for tampering with food.

The Inquisition used more sophisticated methods of water torture, as Scotsman William

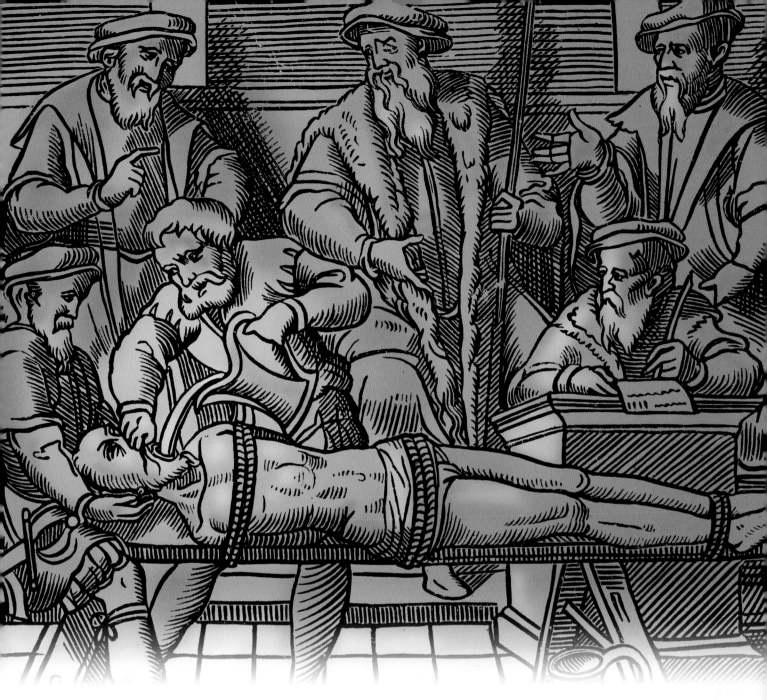

ABOVE: The effect of funneling water down a victim's throat was a painfully rapid expansion of the stomach, followed by a drowning sensation.

Lithgow testified. He had been accused of spying in Spain in 1620 and was stretched on the rack before being force-fed water.

"The first and second [draughts] I gladly received, such was the scorching drought of my tormenting pain, and likewise I had drunk none for three days before. But afterward, at the third charge, perceiving this measure of water to be inflicted on me as tortures, O strangling tortures!"

When he clamped his lips together his mouth was forced open with tools. "My hunger-clung belly waxing great, grew drum-like imbolstred, for it being a suffocating pain, in regard of my head hanging downward and the water reingorging itself, in my throat, with a struggling force, it strangled and swallowed up my breath from yowling and groaning." The technique of force-feeding water to induce the sensation of drowning has been used throughout subsequent centuries and even in modern times.

The Inquisition refined numerous other methods, including slowly dripping water onto the victim's forehead, driving them gradually insane. The Dutch embellished the method by pouring water down the throat of a pinioned victim through a cloth, forcing the material down the throat.

AMPUTATION

Common offenses were punished with uncommon cruelty in the Middle Ages. Mutilation was one way of making sure the punishment fitted the crime.

BELOW: Amputation of the lower leg before the advent of anesthetic. A man with a padded fist stands ready to render the amputee unconscious if he shows signs of reviving, a mercy most did not receive in the Middle Ages.

Minor crimes could send British people to an executioner, who carried out amputations. A pillory or stocks immobilized the victim, although occasionally a fellow was deprived of his limbs while chained up in prison. The lost body part was often appropriate: A thief would lose first a thumb and, for a second offence, the hand that had stolen; a seducer might have his eyes put out; the poacher could lose the feet he had trespassed with.

The suffering of the mutilated was immense. There was no anesthesia so the agony of the ax chop was excruciating. There were no proven medicines, only herbal remedies made by local wise women, so knowledge of the dangers of infection was minimal. Consequently the sentence of amputation was often akin to getting the death penalty, as many died as a consequence of their injury.

Afterward the limbless that survived were associated on sight with villainy. They were unable to find employment, either because they were so incapacitated or they were not trusted, so most continued with crime rather than die of starvation.

Sometimes the law demanded the loss of an ear. King Henry VIII's reign used this as a penalty for non-attendance of church. A felon caught for the second time would lose his other ear. There were cases of victims having their ears nailed to a pillory. The hapless man could only secure his freedom by tearing his own flesh.

MUTILATED FOR LIBEL

While the savagery was usually restricted to general offenses, records show that money-lenders in 1124 had their right hands and testicles cut off, by order of King Henry I. A woman in Portsmouth had her breasts severed.

As the Middle Ages passed, the popularity of amputation waned. However, it was retained as part of the punishment for those considered guilty of libel. When it was used it appeared an anachronism. In 1581 John Stubs, a writer, and William Pace, his publisher, were subjected to public mutilation at Westminster in London after it was deemed they had insulted Queen Elizabeth. Afterward their stumps were cauterized with a hot iron.

An observer wrote: "When his right hand was struck off, [Stubs] plucked off his hat with his left hand and said with a loud voice 'God save the Queen'. The multitude standing about was deeply silent, either out of horror at this new form of punishment or out of commiseration with the man."

As late as 1731 Sir Peter Stringer, who had forged deeds, was subjected to mutilation after a spell in the Charing Cross pillory in London: "…the hangman John Cooper… came up behind him and, with a knife like a gardener's pruning knife, cut off his ears and held them up so that the mob could see them. Having handed them to Mr. Watson, the Sheriff's Officer, the hangman slit both nostrils with a pair of scissors…."

WOUNDED HEELS

Mutilation occurred elsewhere in Europe. In January 1535 French Huguenot (Protestant) Antoine Poile had his tongue pierced and attached to his cheek before being burnt alive. In Russia at the time of Ivan the Terrible it was customary for captured highwaymen to have their heels cut off, or crushed, and be dragged along by their injured ankles. After this torture, most were ready to name their crimes and accomplices and were consequently hanged.

BRANDING

Branding is one of the oldest punishments and was a common part of medieval life. A versatile type of justice, it instantly and indelibly identified the type of criminal.

ENGLISH BRANDING MARKS

Letter	Meaning
B	Blasphemy
F	Fraymaker
M	Manslaughter
P	Perjurer
R	Rogue
S	Slave
SL	Seditious Libeler
SS	Sower of Sedition
T	Thief

Branding dates back to at least 2000 BC, when Babylon was at the height of its power. Greeks, Romans, and Normans all adopted the instant penalty that immediately identified transgressors. In medieval England the system of branding was straightforward, using letter-shaped brands to show the misdemeanor.

The French also scarred criminals. At first the brand was of a fleur de lys, but this was replaced with TF for *travaux forces* (hard labor) and V for *voleur* (thief).

English brands were laid down in a law passed in 1548. By 1624 the punishment was extended to include women. "…Any woman being lawfully convicted by her own confession or by the verdict of 12 good men, of or for the felonious taking of any money, goods, or chattels, above the value of 12 pennies and beneath the value of 10 shillings; or as accessory to any such offence; the said offence not being burglary, nor robbery in or near the highway… shall, for the first offence, be branded and marked in the hand, upon the brawn of the thumb, with a hot burning iron, having a letter 'T' upon it…."

Brandings were administered in open court by the executioner. He might brand the hand, cheek, or shoulder. Having laid the hot iron against bare flesh, causing considerable agony, he inquired of the judge: "A fair mark, my Lord?" If the answer was no, he acted again.

The visible mark rendered people virtually unemployable. Consequently, they turned to a life of crime to sustain themselves and their families.

THE BENEFIT OF CLERGY

While branding gave way to hanging and whipping by the middle of the 14th century, it was retained for a legal loophole. From the 12th century onward clerics accused of misdemeanors in the secular court were permitted to plead "benefit of clergy," which put them before the more lenient ecclesiastical court.

In the reign of Edward III the benefit of clergy was extended to all those clerks, religious or otherwise, who could read. The literacy of the accused was proved by them quoting the 51st psalm, which became known as "the neck verse," because of the number it saved from the noose.

Of course, the system was open to abuse. Education was slowly seeping through society and even the ill-educated could recite the life-saving words from memory. The loophole created an anomaly in English law—the illiterate might be sent to the gallows for seemingly trivial offences, yet those able to read could escape the noose on more serious charges.

The lawmakers responded by restricted the number of offenses to which benefit of clergy could apply. The accused were also branded on the thumb to indicate they had made the plea once. The path to freedom was not offered a second time.

In 1706 the reading test was abolished, having been recognized as meaningless. Benefit of clergy was scrapped in 1790 in the United States and in 1827 in England. In 1779 branding of civilians was abolished in the same act that led to the building of Britain's penitentiaries.

RIGHT: A criminal is branded on the hand in New Sessions' House, London, 1780. Branding was outlawed a decade later in America but remained legal in England—although rarely applied—until 1829.

THE PILLORY

THE STOCKS

A cousin of the pillory was the stocks, which also comprised parallel wooden boards, this time encasing the ankles. The victim was compelled to sit on a stool with his legs outstretched. Again, he was unable to escape the attentions of the crowd. Comical though it may seem today, one of the worst aspects of the punishment was continual tickling on the soles of the feet. The prisoner might also be bodily attacked, and left bruised and battered.

The aim of the pillory was to visit disgrace and shame on criminals in the public gaze. One 20th century wit called it the forerunner of the modern newspaper.

A pillory consisted of two parallel boards, hinged at one side with a central hole for a neck and two for wrists. Once the two boards were pinned together, it was impossible for the victim to escape. Used in France and the USA but particularly popular in Britain, pillories usually stood on platforms to give large crowds a fine view.

Not only could spectators see the pillory and its captive, they were also within throwing range. The hurling of garbage—including vegetables, eggs, stones, feces, dead animals, and shells—was considered part of the punishment. The pillory was mostly used during lunchtimes, when the streets were at their busiest, to increase the victim's burden.

The crowd responded to each case on its merits. Some offenders were guaranteed a rough ride: In 1756 four Englishmen were put in the pillory for falsely claiming rewards after turning in supposed miscreants. The mob knew that the actions of these men had sent innocent people to the gallows. James Egan was dead before the hour's punishment was up. James Salmon, Stephen MacDaniel, and John Berry survived the spell but died from their injuries within days.

Anne Marrow was pilloried in 1777 at London's Charing Cross for marrying three women while posing as a man. Her eyes were put out before she was released; observers noted that women were most incensed by her activities.

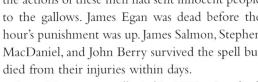

SHIELDED FROM PUNISHMENT

Charles Hitchen, accused of sodomy, was sure of his poor reception and bribed the sheriff. Hitchen wore a suit of armor and a blockade of carts surrounded the pillory, but determined members of the mob clambered toward the terrified man. Only reinforcements summoned by the sheriff saved Hitchen's life. Numerous people were saved by determined police constables on duty around the pillory.

Some victims won the respect and sympathy of the crowd. Famously, writer Daniel Defoe was clapped into the pillory at Charing Cross in 1703 for penning a satire against the Church. He was showered with flowers rather than rocks. The crowd cheered a man pilloried at London's Cheapside for refusing to pay the taxes on soap in 1738.

In 1812 Daniel Eaton was sent to the pillory for publishing Tom Paine, the civil rights advocate. After receiving hearty applause, he was urged to use the pillory to shield his head from the blazing sun. It made the authorities reconsider the use the pillory for people who had won the hearts of ordinary folk. Two years later naval hero Lord Cochrane was saved from his sentence of a spell in the pillory by a government fearful of public antipathy.

The pillory was restricted to those guilty of perjury and subordination after 1816. By 1837 it was abolished entirely in the UK, five years after it was scrapped in France and two years prior to abolition in the United States.

ABOVE: In 1685 anti-Catholic campaigner Titus Oates was found guilty of perjury. The Popish Plot he had concoted, which suggested that Catholics were plotting to assassinate Charles II, led to the deaths of 35 innocent people.

LEFT: Medieval stocks at Painswick in Gloucestershire, England. They rendered the victim immobile, leaving them at the mercy of the mob.

WHIPPING

In medieval England, whipping was a traditional punishment, inflicted upon many people for many reasons. It was frequently a public affair, sometimes with spectators delivering their own blows.

For centuries pupils at English public schools were lashed as a cure-all for impudence, violence, theft, lascivious thoughts, and lewd behavior. As they matured to manhood, victims testified the experience had benefited them and exhorted its use on the next generation.

It was an accepted aspect of worship. An entire spiritual movement had been founded in Europe in the Middle Ages on the basis of self-punishment by birch

BELOW: Whippings by priests were accepted forms of penance.

or thong. The Flagellants sought God's blessing with this overt penance, whipping themselves and each other; the priests whipped all. As part of their vigilant pursuit of heresy the Inquisition also administered floggings.

Children were often taken to public executions and beaten on their return home to ensure the message was received. Men who wished to beat their wives had the law on their side, too, so long as the weapon they wielded was not too hefty. From Tudor times known prostitutes were whipped around the town, tied to the "cart's arse". Vagrants were soundly whipped and returned to their parish if they were caught begging elsewhere. Generally, whipping was considered a just punishment.

Victims were on horseback, on foot attached to a cart, or tied to a fixed pole on a platform, stripped to the waist to compound their shame. Flexing the whip was the local hangman. The condition of both were key: The more braids the whip had, the more painful the punishment, and a strong, mean hangman could deliver more accurate, powerful blows. Those whipped at the cart's tail were lashed for the duration of the journey. In 1736, when a gravedigger was punished for selling bodies for anatomization, an angry mob bribed the hangman to slow the horse. The victim received hundreds of lashes.

ABOVE: Whipping was once an accepted form of punishment for all parts of society. Here the branch of a birch tree is used to punish errant pupils.

WARMING THE SHOULDERS

Floggings in England rarely resulted in death, but in Russia survivors were few. There, executioners used a knout—a wooden-handled whip with braided thongs—which could be frozen or threaded with wire to increase its sting. Whipping was recognized as a death penalty, with the executioner skilled at dislocating his victim's neck at a stroke.

During the British era of the Bloody Codes, whipping was the usual punishment for lesser crimes, including small-time theft, drunkenness on Sunday, rioting, peddling, and seduction. Child offenders were often dealt with in this way. But while age was no barrier, social class certainly was—whipping was for the lower echelons of society, so gentlemen were generally spared the indignity.

It was not unusual to flog women, although some authorities in the late 18th century ordered that the punishment be carried out in private. The notorious Judge Jeffreys advised one hangman on how to deal with a convicted woman: "Scourge her soundly, man, scourge her till her blood runs down! It is Christmas, a cold time for madam to strip. See that you warm her shoulders thoroughly."

Poet Samuel Coleridge was appalled by the public whipping of a woman in 1811. He felt it degraded both victim and punisher. "Good God! How is it possible that man, born of woman, could go through the office? Never let it be forgotten that… the woman is still woman, and however she may have debased herself, yet that she should still shew some respect, still feel some reverence…."

After 1817 women were always whipped behind closed doors. Three years later the punishment was restricted to men until its abolition in Britain in 1862.

TORTURE CHAMBER

"Man is the only one to whom the torture and death of his fellow-creatures is amusing in itself," wrote 19th century historian James Froude in his History of England. *Torturers in Europe amused themselves with a few favored devices.*

That stereotypical fixture of the torture chamber, the rack, first came to Britain around 1420, when the Duke of Exeter was Constable of the Tower of London. Afterward, a spell on the rack was called "being married to the Duke of Exeter's daughter."

The rack was one of the favored options of the Spanish Inquisition, but it was never formally adopted in England as a legal means of obtaining confessions. However, following the discovery of the Gunpowder Plot in 1605, King James I gave his blessing for its application against the captured Guy Fawkes. In a letter to the interrogators the king wrote, "if he will not other wayes confesse, the gentler tortours are to be first usid unto him *et sic per gradus ad ima tenditur* [and so on step by step to the most severe] and so god spede youre goode worke."

Many of the orders for torture in England came from the Star Chamber in the Palace of Westminster, which in Tudor times was devoted to the administration of justice. The victims were accused of treason and included the Knights Templars in the 14th century (see page 80) and active Jesuits in Elizabethan times.

ENFORCED SILENCE

Women in England and Scotland were subjected to the indignities of the scold's bridle or brank, a kind of metal helmet with a gagging strap that prevented them from speaking. A scold was "a troublesome and angry woman who… breaks the public peace, increases discord and becomes a public nuisance." While it was a judge who decided whether a woman was a scold, it was often her husband who testified against her. Women were also plunged into rivers on the ducking stool, a seat dangling from a seesaw beam counterbalanced by an operator using a rope. The shock of the cold water and the length of the ducking were often sufficient to kill.

Elsewhere in Europe the Inquisition used "iron boots" to elicit confessions: With the victim in a sitting position, their feet were tightly bound in a wooden box, then wedges of wood or iron were hammered between box and skin, slicing through the flesh and often breaking bones in the process. Thumbscrews, which probably originated in Russia, were likewise used in Europe. England's King William III tried some for size and declared they would have made him confess to anything.

ENCLOSED AND IMPALED

The Iron Maiden was an upright coffin with inner spikes. When the unfortunate victim was forced inside and the door shut upon them, the spikes strategically pierced organs like the eyes and lungs. However, the prongs were too short to cause rapid death; the prisoner lingered in agony for many hours. England alone made use of the "Skeffington's gyves" or "scavenger's daughter." Dating from Tudor times, it consisted of a metal circle jointed in

two places. The victim knelt on one semi-circle while the torturer forced the other half across their back, tightening it to squash the body.

The Inquisition exceeded the methods of torture employed in Britain. Its implements included white-hot pincers, a heated iron chair, different forms of water torture, hanging by the wrists with weighted ankles, and much more. Bones were crushed, skins slashed, and blood spilled as the Inquisitors sought confessions with the pious intention of saving souls.

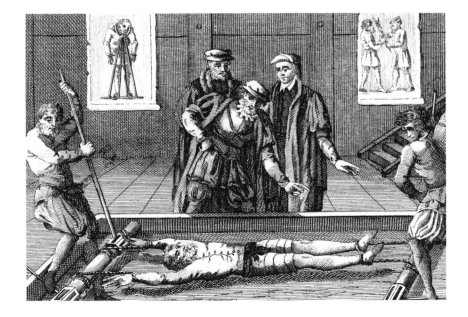

LEFT: A victim is racked as Inquisitors await a confession.

PRESSING TO DEATH

A plea of "guilty" or otherwise was once essential in British trials. There was an advantage in maintaining silence, so the courts crushed the defendant until a response was forthcoming.

By law, defendants in British courts were compelled to plead "guilty" or "not guilty." If the prisoner maintaining a dignified silence, the case could not go ahead, presenting a major dilemma for the authorities.

A legal subtext complicated the issue. Those punished with the death penalty forfeited their estate to the crown, but there was an advantageous loophole for the accused. If he refused to enter a plea, his wealth and property could not be touched, for he would die an unconvicted man. Many were prepared to make the sacrifice to ensure the financial security of the family.

To encourage defendants to plead, the courts employed *peine forte et dure*. When this "strong and hard pain" was defined by law in 1275, it was intended to be hard labor in prison. By 1406 the sentence had been perverted to "pressing to death" and was, for most purposes, a method of execution.

Peine forte et dure was delivered upon a dank cell floor. The accused was spread-eagled, naked but for a loin cloth, with a board placed across the chest and stomach. Day by day, iron weights were piled on the board until the pressure was excruciating, sometimes enough to crush ribs, with fatal results.

The victim might receive three morsels of barley bread on the first day of punishment but no water; on the second day there would be stagnant water but no bread. This went on until the prisoner agreed to plead or died.

Sometimes pieces of wood or jagged stones were placed under the victim's back, a refinement that hastened death. A pebble the size of a cup was put beneath Margaret Clitherow when she was pressed to death at the Tollbooth, outside York's prison cells, on March 25, 1586.

MIRACULOUS ENDURANCE

Clitherow's crime was to be a practicing Catholic when Protestantism was England's prescribed faith. Despite numerous entreaties, she refused to deny Catholicism and a frustrated judge finally sentenced her to be pressed to death. She lay on the open ground, pinned in the shape of a cross, before 800 pounds was piled on top of her. Within 15 minutes she was dead. Margaret was beatified in 1929 and made a saint in 1970.

In the first 20 years of James I's reign 44 people were pressed to death in Middlesex, three of them women. Walter Calverley was pressed to death at York Castle in August 1605. In a fit of insanity he had slaughtered two of his sons and tried to kill his wife at Calverley Hall, Yorkshire. He rode off with the intention of killing his other son, Henry, who was being nursed elsewhere, but Calverley senior was arrested. Overcome with remorse following his incarceration, Calverley refused to plead so that his son might inherit the family home.

At least one man died under weights in Nottingham because he was mute and therefore unable to plead. Remarkably, Cecilia Rygeway survived a pressing of 40 days. Believed to have killed her husband, she wasn't even fed. Ultimately, King

RIGHT: A man is pressed after refusing to plea to a charge of highway robbery. Another weight is about to be added to his burden; compounded with minimal rations, the urge to submit must have been strong, but many died from the weight before they could plead.

Edward III pardoned her, recognizing that her endurance was "after the manner of a miracle and contrary to human nature."

For 366 years pressing to death was a standard punishment in England until the barbaric method was outlawed in 1772. It wasn't until 1827 that silence on behalf of a prisoner was construed as a "not guilty" plea.

WITCH HUNTS IN ENGLAND

ABOVE: Matthew Hopkins, the Witchfinder General, made a lot of money from persecuting solitary women and elderly men.

BELOW: Witches were burned throughout the British Isles. This execution is at the marketplace in Guernsey, the island in the English Channel.

Beggars in England posed as witches to get more money but risked the attention of witchfinders. These men, typified by Matthew Hopkins, used dubious means to define witchcraft and hanged the guilty.

Between 1558, when Elizabeth I took the throne, and 1736, when witchcraft was no longer an offense, 513 cases of witchcraft were scrutinized in the Courts of the Home Circuit, which covered five southern counties. The result was 200 convictions and 109 hangings.

The victims tended to be solitary old women. Those who were widowed and/or childless were among the most vulnerable in society. They were forced to beg to survive, and sometimes it suited them to be considered witches, as it could inspire greater generosity. Some women claimed they caused blizzards, frosts, storms, and so forth to enhance their reputation.

Women like these were likely to keep cats or even frogs that could be seen as "familiars," on loan from the devil to assist in evil spells. Warts, moles, and other marks were interpreted as "devil's teats."

These were not enlightened times; belief in superstition, lucky charms, and evil spirits was widespread. People sought a scapegoat for misfortune, and women acting as witches often took the blame. Accusations tended toward the petty; the sentence of hanging was not. It remained difficult for the accused to prove they did not issue a curse or spell.

Getting a confession was far from easy. Matthew Hopkins, the notorious Witchfinder General, used psychological more than physical torture, depriving people of food, drink, and sleep until they admitted their guilt as a witch. A 70-year-old, John Lowes, was forced to run around his cell, finally collapsing and admitting guilt after three days. Lowes was sent to the gallows, where he recited his own burial service.

INNOCENCE IN DEATH

Hopkins illustrated how witches were impervious to pain by stabbing them with a knife—the blade was retractable so the victim didn't feel a thing. He had the backing of zealous Puritans who took to heart the line in Exodus, "Thou shalt not suffer a witch to live."

For 14 months Hopkins was the scourge of witches, welcomed into towns all over eastern England, outside the Home Circuit. His tally at the gallows amounted to some 400. Hopkins' methods were exposed as fraudulent but not before he became a rich man. Legend says that Hopkins was tried and burned as a witch; today it is thought he died in 1647, possibly of tuberculosis, soon after retiring to Manningtree, Essex, the town where his career had begun.

The law endorsed various methods to identify the guilty, such as "swimming" witches. The unfortunate woman was tossed into a river. If she floated she was a witch, as the (baptismal) waters had rejected her. If she drowned she was innocent.

Left in the hands of rural communities, the women often suffered more appalling abuses. It was said that witches' power waned once their blood had been drawn. Consequently, unruly mobs made it their business to leave suspected witches bloodied.

Devout Christian Reginald Scot campaigned against the harassment of so-called witches. As early as 1583 he wrote *Discoverie of Witchcraft*, ridiculing the public perception. "If you read the executions done upon witches, you shall see such impossibilities confessed as none, having his right wits, will believe."

Skepticism at last had its day. The small voices that had questioned the validity of witchfinders' methods during the Elizabethan era grew ever louder until legislation ended the witch trials. In 1712 Jane Wenham, the subject of the last witch trial in England, was reprieved and pardoned when the girl she allegedly bewitched was found to be an epileptic.

Above: A public hanging in 1678 claimed the lives of seven women accused of witchcraft.

THE SALEM SENSATION

"We walked in clouds and could not see our way." So said the Rev John Hale as he tried to make sense of Salem's departure from common sense into the realms of evil fantasy.

Salem, Massachusetts was transformed into a hellhole of denunciation and death at the say-so of children. One man was pressed to death and 19 were hanged before sanity returned. A day of mourning was declared and no one in America was ever pressed to death again.

The nightmare began in the early months of 1692, when a small group of girls listened to tales of magic told by Tituba, a Carib slave woman in the service of local minister Samuel Parris. The insight Tituba gave them into a hot and vivid world flustered these impressionable girls and they became hysterical.

When they were quizzed by adults, the girls—Abigail Williams, 11, Ann Putnam, 12, and 9-year-old Betty Parris—claimed they had been bewitched by three local women. These were Tituba, a humble beggar called Sarah Good, and a widow, Sarah Osburne, all outsiders in this close-knit and devout community. Tituba was black, Good smoked a pipe, and Osburne had lived in sin before marrying her second husband; none attended church.

Tituba confessed under interrogation, giving the same titillating detail that had so excited the children's interest. She was allowed to go free, but the town's dignitaries became convinced that an epidemic of witches had spread through the community. More than 400 people were arrested as they tried to root them out.

One of them was five-year-old Dorcas Good, daughter of Sarah, who was chained up in jail for seven months. Sarah was hanged. Constable John Willard was sentenced to death after he refused to make further arrests.

BELOW: Witch trials were held in several places in America, but Salem remains the most notorious.

UNLIKELY ACCUSATIONS

Innkeeper Bridget Bishop was accused of transforming herself into a bizarre creature with the body of a monkey, feet of a rooster, and face of a man, then haunting innocent men at night.

Rev. George Burroughs was accused of seducing young girls into sorcery. Harvard graduate Burroughs was a former pastor in Salem who left following a parish quarrel. He was arrested at his new post in Wells, Maine and brought back to face trial, where he was accused of being a ringleader of witches. It was said he caused the deaths of the wife and daughter of his successor. An inspection of his teeth convinced observers that he was responsible for bite marks on young girls.

It was 80-year-old Giles Cory who was pressed to death. He refusal to plead to charges of witchcraft, without which he could not be

examined in court. He was taken to a field where rocks were heaped upon his chest in an attempt to make him concede. Cory died in agony.

The court proceedings make bizarre reading. There were numerous mentions of the Black Man, as the devil was known, with elaborate descriptions of ritual, psychic episodes, and feats of strength all attributed to Satanic intervention. In the dock witnesses frequently showed symptoms of bewitchment, causing further chaos.

One account relates how "It cost the Court a wonderful deal of trouble, to hear the testimonies of the sufferers, for when they were going to give in their depositions, they would for a long time be taken with fits, that made them incapable of saying anything. The Chief Judge asked the prisoner who he thought hindered these witnesses from giving their testimonies? And he answers, he supposes it was the Devil. That honorable person then replied, how comes the Devil so loathe to have any testimony borne against you? Which cast him into very great confusion."

PAPAL INQUISITION

In the medieval world all bowed down to God's temporal representative, the Pope. The Inquisition was formed to maintain his power, but its methods and motives ran out of control.

The Pope's authority was beyond question and some of the most barbarous torture and executions of the Middle Ages took place in his name. The Pope was constantly fearful of losing his grip on power. His mandate was forceful enough and both rich and poor were concerned for their spirituality, but representatives of the Catholic Church were not above misusing their influence. Many had a reputation for greed, which in turn sparked a ground swell of opposition. When alternatives to Catholicism presented themselves they attracted surprisingly large followings. The Cathari sect, from Bulgaria, spread over southern Europe in the 11th century, while the Waldensians began challenging Papal authority in the 13th century. Excommunication was no longer enough to keep the flock in line.

The Pope's response was the institution of the Holy Office or Inquisition. Formalized in 1231 by Pope Gregory IX, the Inquisition's task was to deal with heretics—those who veered from Papal dogma—as well as moral crimes.

Spaniard St. Dominic inspired a new order, the Dominicans, founded in 1216. St. Francis of Assisi had started his own order six years previously. Devout, pious, and zealous Dominican and Franciscan friars proved to be the men for the job.

By 1252 the use of torture had been sanctioned in order to elicit confessions. Those in the clutches of the Inquisition were taken to the brink of despair by the brutality wielded against them.

THE INQUISITION'S STRATEGY

Inquisition parties marched from place to place, carrying large crucifixes to telegraph their ominous presence. Following their arrival, heretics and other offenders had a month in which to give themselves up. Those who readily confessed were welcomed back into the arms of the Catholic Church after a penance.

Then the friars turned their attentions to those denounced as heretics by local church people or envious neighbors. Just two witnesses were enough to convince the Inquisitors of guilt. Bribery or the threat of torture could secure those witnesses.

Then interrogation began. The friars had horrible mechanisms at their disposal, including the rack, the strappado—which stretched the limbs of the victim

with weights—the iron boot, thumbscrews, whips, and brands. There was no defense system and anyone who supported the victim was also condemned as a heretic.

The wealth and estates of convicted heretics funded the Inquisitors, therefore the moneyed classes were targeted. Most at risk were sincere, moneyed Catholics wrongly accused of heresy who felt unable to confess, despite the appalling and painful indignities confronting them. Those found guilty were handed over to the secular authorities to be burned at the stake.

Although the Inquisition relented in the rest of Europe after the 14th century, it gained renewed impetus in Spain. Tomas de Torquemada was the black-hearted Grand Inquisitor in Spain from 1483. His primary targets were Jewish people, who became Christians following the bleak "convert or quit" edict in 1492. Muslims that remained in Spain, particularly Granada, were other targets for the Inquisition.

BOTTOM LEFT: A procession of heretics approach a Grand Inquisitor. They are led up steps beyond him and tied to stakes, ready for burning.

BELOW: Torturers try to force a confession from the Inquisitors' victim. The guilty were burned at the stake.

A New World

Capital punishment—the ultimate deterrent—underpinned the correction of crime across the world until the 18th century. In Britain a man could be sentenced to death for robbing a rabbit warren or marrying a Jew. In 1766 Charles-Henri Sanson beheaded a man in France who failed to hail some passing monks. There was virtually no other recognized remedy for villainy, no matter how petty the misdemeanor.

Then came the Enlightenment. It had ramifications for religion, philosophy, politics, and even art. Crucially it challenged the accepted beliefs surrounding crime and punishment. Charles de Montesquieu, one of the French luminaries of the Enlightenment, began to question the wholesale human destruction that prevailed across Europe.

Inspired by Montesquieu, Italian criminologist Cesare Beccaria set out his forward-looking theories in "Crimes and Punishments," an essay published in 1764. It was the first comprehensive account of the principles that governed law. Beccaria came to the inescapable conclusion that both torture and the death penalty were wrong. He argued that long-term imprisonment was a more powerful discouragement because execution was a fleeting spectacle.

Other voices made themselves heard in this Age of Reason: David Hume in Scotland, Gotthold Lessing in Germany, Voltaire and Rousseau in France, and Benjamin Franklin and Thomas Jefferson in the American colonies. While it was Beccaria who focussed specifically on crime and punishment, they all spoke of basic human rights and tolerance with just government.

Although it took years, the ideas diffused into society, despite attacks by the Church and local censorship. The abuses suffered, particularly by the burgeoning working classes created in the Industrial Revolution, were still immense. However, the seeds of doubt that would lead to reform had been sown.

RIGHT: Decapitation by guillotine, the most infamous method of execution, was created in a simpler form centuries before its heyday in Revolutionary France. King Louis XVI's severed head was shown to the crowd that gathered for his death on 21 January 1793.

POOR HOUSES

Traditionally Christians were supposed to cherish the poor, glory in charity, and value humility. By Tudor times this Biblical tenet was turned on its head and poor people were reviled and distrusted.

The poor faced a dilemma after the dissolution of the monasteries under Henry VIII, which once provided food and shelter. Now those in the rapidly growing urban areas who faced the perils of disease and starvation in the absence of charity had no option but to thieve.

A remedy was provided in London, 1553, by the largesse of King Edward VI. Ten days before his untimely death, the sickly 17-year-old donated the royal palace at Bridewell "for to be a workhouse for the poor and idle persons of the city of London."

His successor, Queen Mary I, delayed ratification of the necessary charter, but finally Bridewell became a hospital, a home for the poor, and a place of correction. The notion was noble enough but in practice Bridewell became a punishment for the poor. The pioneering paternalism was fatally flawed, but only future generations would appreciate its problems.

Organized relief of the poor was not a new idea and Bridewell was not the first institution of its kind. Humanist Juan Vives from Spain had advocated increased levels of relief for the poor. In Amsterdam the Rasp House was established in the 1550s to house vagrants. However, Bridewell became a warts-and-all model for the rest of England to follow, even lending its name to similar institutions.

Bridewell became home to orphans and children of the poor, the sick or crippled, and able-bodied vagrants. They were given work, including silk-winding, wool-carding, cap- and nail-making. In return they earned a small wage and generated a profit for Bridewell.

BELOW: The female ward of St. James' Parish Workhouse, a descendant of the original Bridewell in London.

KEPT IN WORK

Not everyone was enamoured with the idea. Mary I had grave reservations about its very existence, perhaps because prostitutes within Bridewell spoke freely about their liaisons with Catholic priests. Sir Francis Bacon felt that caging the poor was against the spirit of the Magna Carta and contrary to English ethos.

Those operating Bridewell were tempted to let "women of ill repute" start up business to generate further income. The managers who took over in 1602 kicked out most of the paupers and let the rooms for a fee instead, to increase their profits.

Nevertheless, following the Poor Law of 1572, Bridewells or houses of correction were established all over England. By 1609 local justices were liable to a £5 fine if they had not provided a house of correction where the poor could be "as straitly kept in diet as in work."

Vagrants were rounded up and committed to Bridewells, where they were usually whipped on arrival. Whipping became such a common punishment in London's Bridewell that a gallery was specially built to accommodate fee-paying spectators. There was a pillory too, sometimes a ducking stool, and many residents were kept in irons.

Distinction between the poor and criminal classes became vague. With pressure mounting on jails, the justices sent convicted felons to houses of correction, which consequently became fortified in a bid to keep criminals in.

The concept was reinterpreted in the second half of the 18th century when nine huge Houses of Industry were built in Britain to provide labor and shelter for the poor. Once inside, people were compelled to wear uniforms and the doors were locked. Bridewells were still going strong in the 19th century, although by then their small profits made them unpopular investments.

CLAPPED IN IRONS

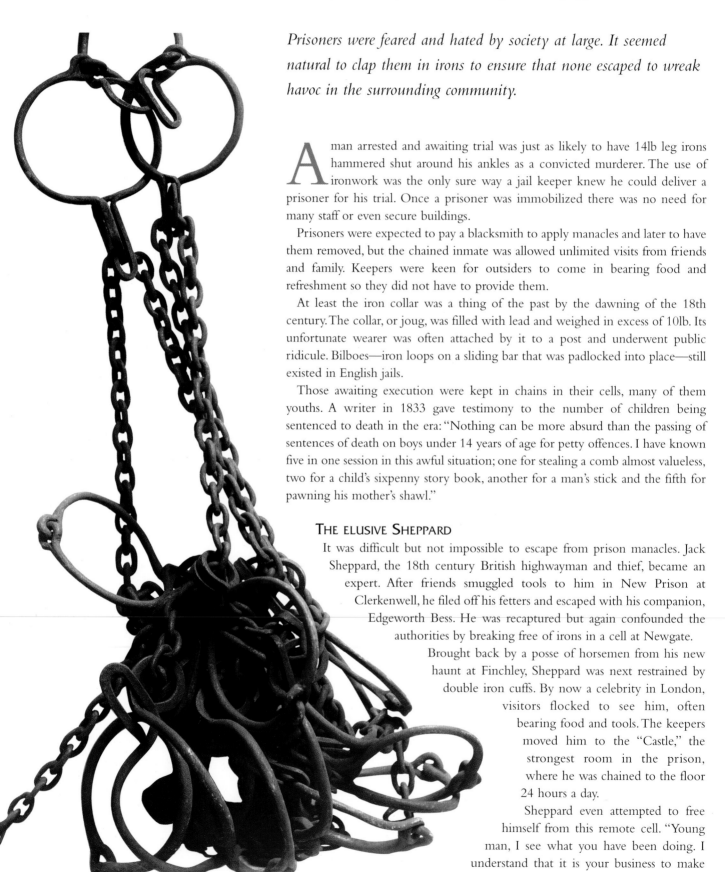

Prisoners were feared and hated by society at large. It seemed natural to clap them in irons to ensure that none escaped to wreak havoc in the surrounding community.

A man arrested and awaiting trial was just as likely to have 14lb leg irons hammered shut around his ankles as a convicted murderer. The use of ironwork was the only sure way a jail keeper knew he could deliver a prisoner for his trial. Once a prisoner was immobilized there was no need for many staff or even secure buildings.

Prisoners were expected to pay a blacksmith to apply manacles and later to have them removed, but the chained inmate was allowed unlimited visits from friends and family. Keepers were keen for outsiders to come in bearing food and refreshment so they did not have to provide them.

At least the iron collar was a thing of the past by the dawning of the 18th century. The collar, or joug, was filled with lead and weighed in excess of 10lb. Its unfortunate wearer was often attached by it to a post and underwent public ridicule. Bilboes—iron loops on a sliding bar that was padlocked into place—still existed in English jails.

Those awaiting execution were kept in chains in their cells, many of them youths. A writer in 1833 gave testimony to the number of children being sentenced to death in the era: "Nothing can be more absurd than the passing of sentences of death on boys under 14 years of age for petty offences. I have known five in one session in this awful situation; one for stealing a comb almost valueless, two for a child's sixpenny story book, another for a man's stick and the fifth for pawning his mother's shawl."

THE ELUSIVE SHEPPARD

It was difficult but not impossible to escape from prison manacles. Jack Sheppard, the 18th century British highwayman and thief, became an expert. After friends smuggled tools to him in New Prison at Clerkenwell, he filed off his fetters and escaped with his companion, Edgeworth Bess. He was recaptured but again confounded the authorities by breaking free of irons in a cell at Newgate.

Brought back by a posse of horsemen from his new haunt at Finchley, Sheppard was next restrained by double iron cuffs. By now a celebrity in London, visitors flocked to see him, often bearing food and tools. The keepers moved him to the "Castle," the strongest room in the prison, where he was chained to the floor 24 hours a day.

Sheppard even attempted to free himself from this remote cell. "Young man, I see what you have been doing. I understand that it is your business to make good your escape, if you can, and it is mine to take care you shall not," said the jailer. "Then let us both look to our business," replied the indomitable Jack.

On October 15, 1724 Sheppard escaped the Castle, still wearing the leg irons that he had filed from their housings. Alas his bragging brought about his recapture. Jack Sheppard was held in outsized chains by the ankle and wrist during his final stay in Newgate and eventually hanged.

Chain gangs also left prison hulks (pages 108–109) to work the land in fetters. A survey of prisons carried out by London merchant James Neild in 1812 found that the routine use of chains had been largely abandoned except at the chronically overcrowded and old-fashioned Newgate, which reserved them for the most quarrelsome and violent prisoners.

BOTTOM LEFT: For the more slippery and notorious criminals, a cell wasn't enough; they were also chained to a wall or floor.

BELOW: Jack Sheppard became notorious for his escapes. This portrait was first sketched during his final stay in Newgate Prison.

ASYLUMS

In a society that relished pastimes like bear-baiting and cock-fighting, it is not surprising that Elizabethans found amusement in the antics of the insane. Fair and understanding treatment of the mentally ill was centuries away.

Bethlehem Hospital, better known as Bedlam, was founded in 1274 as a priory. It became a hospital by 1330 and began admitting mental patients in 1403. In 1557 it came under the direct control of Bridewell (see pages 90–91); the following year it issued this edict: "Be it known to all devout and faithful people that there have been erected in the city of London four hospitals for the people that be stricken by the hand of God. Some be distraught from their wits and these be kept and maintained in the Hospital of Our Lady of Bedlam, until God call them to his mercy or to their wits again."

BELOW: Bedlam, from Hogarth's revealing series of pictures from the era. Patients were subjected to all manner of indignities that were savored by fee-paying audiences.

Quack treatment prevailed. Pope John XXI concocted some of the more dubious recipes in the 13th century. He urged physicians to cut the liver from a frog, fold it in a colewort leaf, and burn it in a new earthen pot, mixing the ashes with good wine to administer to the poor lunatic. He also believed it efficacious to eat roasted mice.

The well-intentioned Elizabethan Andrew Boorde urged the use of "mirth and merry communication." It is doubtful that there was much laughter in Bedlam. The keepers' usual response to symptoms of insanity was to administer a beating. Not surprisingly, the word "bedlam" came to mean "scene of uproar" and was synonymous with cruelty and neglect.

Admission to Bedlam was not regulated. Unscrupulous guardians might commit their rich but feeble-minded charges to it, and husbands would leave problem wives there.

ENLIGHTENMENT DAWNS

Bedlam was positioned between two sewers. In 1598 one visitor wrote: "It was so loathsomely filthily kept that it was not fit for any man to come into." That did not keep paying visitors away.

They joined in verbal abuse and watched in fascination as the insane were whipped. Records indicate that Bedlam's patients were occasionally rented out as a floorshow, the proceeds going to the keepers.

It was years before the public's attitude toward the mentally afflicted changed. A report in *The Times* of 1816 registered a fresh response. It criticized the practice of keeping the insane strapped in straitjackets for weeks at a time and the employment of harsh keepers. It called for purpose-built, general asylums to replace "those stone, unwindowed, unchimnied, parish pigsties of cold, filth and vermin, where lunacy now has its wretched abode."

"Let [England's] humanity and good sense call to mind, that the madman is still a man with all his rights unforfeited; and that though the mental rays are distorted, the sensations are no less vivid."

In France in 1792 the superintendent of a Parisian asylum struck the irons off its inmates, insisting that chains merely constrained the body and discipline was necessary to order the mind. This fiercely moral conviction was adopted by Quakers in England and by doctor and philanthropist Benjamin Rush in America.

Believing crime and insanity to be medical problems, Rush built "the tranquilizer," a chair with built-in commode and wooden blinkers to restrain patients who had fallen into a frenzy. He also invented "the gyrator," a table onto which patients were strapped and spun at high speed, to shock the brain into normal thought. Both were abandoned when reluctant patients were injured while they were steered toward the dreadful contraptions.

ABOVE: A disturbed woman prisoner at Woking jail is confined in a padded cell.

SILENT AND SOLITARY CONFINEMENT

"Solitude and silence are favorable to reflection and may possibly lead to repentance," declared prison reformer John Howard. With these words he condemned hundreds of prisoners to a solitary existence that destroyed their spirit and threatened their sanity.

ALONE IN ALCATRAZ

In the 20th century solitary confinement was used as a punishment rather than a cure. At Alcatraz, California's island jail between 1934 and 1963 that housed Al Capone and "birdman" Robert F. Stroud, the solitary cell used for errant prisoners was known as "the Hole." One inmate described it as "a private purgatory where carefully chosen victims are slowly driven mad."

John Howard was dead by the time the Rule of Silence was imposed on Britain, carried off by gaol fever while inspecting prisons of the Crimea. Although well-meaning, in practice his rule was a harsh punishment.

Behind the desire to impose silence upon prisoners was the level of noise in 18th century jails that left inmates unable to ponder the error of their ways. Clergymen were convinced that silence, like that established in monasteries, was necessary for contemplation and rehabilitation. It would also end the tradition of an old prisoner tutoring a young felon in methods of crime.

Britain was finally pushed into adopting silent association after witnessing its effect in the American prisons of Auburn and Sing-Sing. In Philadelphia's Eastern State Penitentiary, opened in 1829 at a cost of $780,000, prisoners were held in solitary confinement for up to five years. Such sentences were rejected in England as too cruel.

All conversation between prisoners was banned at Coldbath Fields House of Correction in London in 1834, the first of 20 English jails to take the momentous step. The governor at Coldbath Fields reported: "Prisoners are kept under constant and secret inspection day and night… every movement of the prisoners is made so as to prevent their faces being turned to each other, they are never allowed to congregate or cluster together, they move in solitary lines in single file."

SILENT AND ANONYMOUS

To drive the message home prisoners were masked and tagged, so they were known only by a number. Women donned black veils and likewise wore a tag. The aim was to prevent prisoners from recognizing each other.

Speech was punished by a flogging or a bread and water diet. Even a whisper was enough to earn a spell in the punishment block known as the dark cells. Instead, inmates adopted secret codes, including hand signals and pipe tapping.

One letter and one visit were permitted for prisoners every six months. They suffered delusions, depression, and sometimes madness. Charles Dickens was against silent association. "I hold this slow and daily tampering with the mysteries of the brain to be immeasurably worse than any torture of the body."

In 1835 Elizabeth Fry spoke out against prisons of the day: "In some respects, I think there is more cruelty in our gaols than I have ever before seen." It was nevertheless a golden age for prisons. In Britain the model prison Pentonville was opened in 1842, Australia's largest building, the Penitentiary at Port Arthur, was completed the same year, and in France prisoners were given meager wages in return for menial work.

The failing condition of prisoners' mental health eventually caused a re-think about silence in prisons in Britain, as it had done in America. Solitary confinement was officially abandoned in Easter State Penitentiary in 1913, although in reality it had broken down years before.

BOTTOM LEFT: Rows of prisoners work silently at Coldbath Fields, their name and identity replaced by a number.

BELOW: John Howard was appalled when he visited jails under his jurisdiction, but silent confinement was little kinder than solitary.

AUSTRALIA

With its prisons bulging, Britain was keen to establish another penal colony. America was no longer open to convicts and slaves were a cheaper, less troublesome form of labor for the West Indies. An island off the African coast was thought too precarious. Established colonialists in both Nova Scotia and the Cape of Good Hope objected to having Britain's criminals thrust upon them.

Joseph Banks, president of the Royal Society, had been with James Cook on his world voyage when Australia's east coast was claimed for Britain. Appreciating the possibilities, Banks told the government it could be a colony "larger than the whole of Europe." The cost of transportation would be high but few would have the opportunity to illegally return. Ministers decided that Australia was a perfect place of exile.

When Australia became the new destination for criminals, it was literally the great unknown. Given the disease, heat, and voracious insect life, the "savages" that Sarah Mills had been afraid of in 1786—the aborigines—would be the least of her problems.

The "First Fleet" was gathered by Captain Arthur Philip, a retired naval man who would be governor of the new colony. It comprised 11 ships, six of them transports for convicts. He made every effort to ensure there were sufficient provisions aboard for his men and the 736 male and female convicts, but was thwarted by a government keen to economize.

RIGHT: The Aborigines native to Australia were as unprepared for the new arrivals as the transportees were for the inhospitable conditions. Many died from the diseases that the Westerners found relatively harmless.

SICKENED BY THE BRITISH

Curiosity got the better of the aborigines who initially threw spears at the landing parties. All aspects of the visitors' lifestyles were a revelation to the aborigines, from guns to boiling pots. The newcomers also brought diseases, including flu and typhus, that soon decimated the native population. The aborigines began pilfering small items but the convicts were barred from taking revenge. Although Philip insisted on cordial relations with the aborigines, distrust remained on both sides, eventually boiling over into conflict.

ESTABLISHING SYDNEY

Before the fleet sailed on May 12, 1787 17 convicts died in the holds of the ships, following an outbreak of gaol fever. The prisoners were held in large cages in darkness—there were no portholes and lamps were barred. Daylight came from hatchways above, but these were battened down in bad weather.

When the ships were at sea the convicts were allowed to exercise on deck; when they were in dock prisoners were confined to their stale, vermin-ridden quarters. The fleet stopped for a week at Tenerife, a month in Rio de Janeiro, and a further month in Cape Town.

It wasn't until January 19, 1788 that the ships berthed in Botany Bay. Philip felt the dense vegetation was unsuitable and struck out around the coast, preferring the shores at Sydney Cove.

Of the 48 people who died *en route*, 40 were convicts and five were their children (the youngest of the felons was 9-year-old John Hudson). One of the survivors was Dorothy Handland, aged 82, convicted of perjury. After arrival in Australia she hung herself from a gum tree.

Between 1787 and 1852 an estimated 150,000 convicts were transported to eastern Australia. Tasmania received a further 37,000 before transportation there was halted in 1853. Prisoners were dispatched to the hostile reaches of western Australia until 1868. A fifth of all transportees did not survive the journey.

ABOVE: A convict bids farewell to relatives; a row boat awaits to take him to a ship that will make the long journey to the unknown territory of Australia.

DEVIL'S ISLAND

France also had penal colonies, although on a much smaller scale than Britain. French jails were chronically overcrowded. In 1852 Louis Napoleon III decided to exploit overseas colonies where, he anticipated, convicts could reflect on their crimes and reform. Consequently "Le Bagne" (convict prison) was created in French Guiana in South America, 3,000 miles from home.

Lying at about five degrees north of the equator, French Guiana was dominated by steamy jungle and its associated hazards. There were the usual privations of inadequate food, poor sanitation, and a lack of medical care. Of the 70,000 prisoners dispatched there, approximately 50,000 perished.

Although operating under the surveillance of guards, there was some degree of freedom. However, standards soon degenerated with gambling, homosexual rape, violence, and even murder rife in the dormitory cells that held the men at night.

Those who killed guards or their families faced the guillotine. Anyone found guilty of murdering a fellow convict was sent to one of the logging camps established in the heart of the jungle or, in the worst instances, to Devil's Island. It was also the destination for political dissidents

Devil's Island was the collective name given to three small rocky outcrops in the Atlantic Ocean, 20 miles off the coast of French Guiana, once containing leper colonies. The largest of the islands, Ile Royale, is just under two miles wide.

A DOUBLE SENTENCE

On the Ile de St Joseph was the dreaded reclusion block, known as the dry guillotine. The most troublesome convicts spent their days and nights there in silence, without books, pens, or paper, under the constant gaze of patrolling guards. One of the inmates, Rene Belbenoit, described it as being "alive in a tomb."

The opportunities for escape were slim, but this did not stop Belbenoit from trying. Not only did he flee the inhospitable island, by raft and hand-hewn canoe, but he also survived the punishments that awaited him when his attempts failed. He finally won his freedom after digging out a tree trunk to make a canoe and paddling 700 miles to Trinidad.

Little-publicized legislation meant few would return from Devil's Island. The Law of Doubling meant that those with a sentence of less than eight years had to follow it with a similar spell in Guiana, where they tried, but often failed, to earn their passage home. Anyone with a sentence of more than eight years had to spend the rest of their days in the colony. After 1885 only criminals with sentences of more than eight years were sent to Devil's Island.

Following a visit from a journalist in 1923 a scandal about conditions in Le Bagne erupted. By 1928 the government had dispatched the Salvation Army. Officers were appalled by the conditions and the dilemma facing those that were freed yet unable to find work. By 1938 Devil's Island was abandoned; Le Bagne was closed entirely by 1954. In an attempt to obliterate its sorry history, the French have now renamed the outcrops Les Iles du Salut—The Islands of Salvation.

LEFT: Alfred Dreyfuss was persecuted by the higher echelons of the French army and faced an inflated spying charge. He battled to keep his sanity on Devil's Island.

HULKS

A hulk ship, the Defence, *was destroyed in a fire in 1857; the hospital hulk* Unite *was emptied soon after. Thus a woeful chapter in Britain's penal history closed.*

ABOVE: A warder watches prisoners file into their cells on the *Warrior*, a hulk moored at Woolwich. It held 600 prisoners, who were sometimes released for use as cheap labor at a government dockyard.

Britain siphoned off some of her most irksome citizens to America by way of transportation. Typically those transported had won a reprieve from the death sentence or were considered too inconsequential to hang.

When America no longer accepted the flotsam of British society after 1775, the government found itself with large numbers of convicts on its hands. The following year a temporary solution was agreed "for the more severe and effectual punishment of atrocious and daring offenders," that of the hulks. Today that name is symbolic of all that was squalid in the system of punishments in Britain in the late 18th and early 19th centuries.

Hulks were decrepit warships moored first on the River Thames at Woolwich, London and later at Chatham, Portsmouth, Gosport, Plymouth, and Deptford. The ships had been bought by Duncan Campbell, the entrepreneur charged with operating the hulks to be used as prisoner accommodation. Campbell received £38 per year for every prisoner, from the government. From this he paid guards and took a tidy profit. He reinvested little of the money in the ships so the living conditions were cramped and insanitary.

Prisoners sentenced to transportation found themselves on hulks as they awaited a passage, or were held there for a prescribed number of years as their sentence. Two brothers aged 11 and nine were sent to the prison hulk *Euryalis* in Chatham to await transportation for "taking a chain out of a cart." The elder boy died; the fate of the other is unknown.

By day the convicts undertook hard labor like building docks or raising gravel from riverbeds. This satisfied one lobby, which had long thought that convict labor should directly benefit Britain rather than her colonies. From the prisoner's point of view, at least they were outside enjoying fresh air.

BREEDING GROUNDS FOR SICKNESS AND CRIME

At night the hatches were battened down with the men, women, and children in the bowels of the creaking ships. Guards admitted they rarely entered prisoner quarters after dark, and then only in armed parties. Alcohol-fuelled violence was largely left to erupt undisturbed.

Disease was rife, including gaol fever (see page 85) and cholera. Few doctors could be tempted aboard to tend the sick; the death rate was estimated at one in four. Reformer John Howard inspected the hulk *Justitia* in 1776. "Many [convicts] had no shirts, some no waistcoats… some no stockings and some no shoes." He witnessed those about to die and many that yearned for death as a release.

Although the ships were secure, prisoners sometimes escaped, and caused havoc in the densely populated ports where the hulks were moored. It became apparent that hardened criminals aboard the hulks were educating the young in enterprising methods of crime. Yet although the drawbacks were numerous, the hulks survived for some 80 years. By 1787 there were 2,000 convicts aboard them.

After visiting a hulk at Chatham in 1828 to see her husband (whose crime is not recorded), a woman asked a vicar to intercede and ask the Home Secretary to secure his freedom. "I found him in great distress drawing timber on a cart like a horse. He thinks it a very hard case that he is thus compelled to suffer… when he has done nothing but spoken the truth in defense of the laws of the nation. There is no law for a poor man."

BELOW: The hulk at Deptford was typical, providing ramshackle accommodation for hardened convicts, erring women, and even misguided children.

HANGMEN

To Londoners, all hangmen went by nickname Jack Ketch. Yet the skills and qualities of the city's executioners varied considerably.

Jack Ketch took the post of London's executioner in 1663 and gained infamy after butchering Lord William Russell and the Duke of Monmouth with an ax, the mode of execution for upper classes. After his tenure, hangmen were known as Ketch, or alternatively Lord of the Scaffold, Finisher of the Law, Yeoman of the Halter, Doomster, or Scragboy.

Each successive hangman brought different talents to the task. John Hooper, who took on the role in London between 1728 and 1735, was known for making jokes to alleviate the victim's burden. From 1752 Thomas Turlis had to bear the wrath of the mob when it was ruled that convicts' bodies should go to surgeons. He died from injuries sustained in a tussle at Tyburn in 1771.

His successor Edward Dennis—on whom Charles Dickens based Barnaby Rudge—was almost hanged when he was convicted of taking part in riots in London. He was reprieved only because his services were sorely needed to dispense justice to the numerous felons rounded up in the Gordon riots of 1780.

Dennis's assistant, William Brunskill, was elevated to the post and remained there for 28 years. It fell to him to hang John Bellingham, the assassin of Prime Minister Spencer Perceval in 1812. He was broadly abused by the assembled crowd, for Bellingham was seen as a hero striking a blow against a corrupt, uncaring government.

Brunskill eventually succumbed to ill health; his promoted assistant John Langley lasted only a few years, dying at the age of 51.

PROFIT IN DEATH

William Calcraft held the job for 45 years. This became a black era for prisoners, as Calcraft had a reputation for bungling. The ropes he used were short so he often had to swing on the man's legs to speed up the hanging process. Afterward he retrieved the rope for future use. His most positive contribution was a belt with wrist straps for the hanged; previously their bindings were often uncomfortably tight.

At the hanging of Thomas and Maria Mannings in 1849 Calcraft was either nervous or drunk. Writer Charles Dickens clearly believed it was the latter when he commented, "Mr. Calcraft, the hangman, should be restrained in his unseemly briskness, in his jokes, his oaths and his brandy."

Hangmen made a tidy sum by selling lengths of rope that had hanged the famous or infamous. Superstition had it that the touch of a recently hanged man's hand possessed miraculous healing powers. The death sweat was said to cure

BELOW: This hangman caricature from 1840, subtitled "A ridiculous superfluity," expresses anti-execution sentiment in a humorous way.

tuberculosis, while the hand was attributed with sufficient potency to cure infertility in women and reduce tumors. For cash the hangman allowed the afflicted to mount the scaffold and clutch the cooling hand of the dead.

An executioner might even sever the hand of the victim to sell to the highest bidder. The "hand of glory" was sometimes dried and pickled by an aspiring burglar, since it was believed it could render them invisible.

In France the clothes of the guillotined were washed and given to the poor. In England they became the property of the hangman. Great store was set by looking elegant, so this was quite a bonus. In 1752 William Signal sold his body to surgeons so he could buy fashionable clothes in which to die.

BELOW: Longstanding hangman William Calcraft was the executioner at Britain's last public hanging (see pages 116–117).

CHEATING THE GALLOWS

Gathered around the foot of the scaffold were mothers, brothers, and sweethearts of the convicted, hoping for miracle. By fate or unusual endurance, some got their wish.

ABOVE: James Berry and the wardens assisting him were confused when the gallows' trapdoor refused to open.

Sometimes those sent to hang were saved by a last-minute reprieve, delivered with the thundering arrival of a messenger on horseback. There was the possibility that the accused would somehow survive the hanging. Many attempted resuscitation of the cut-down victims; few were successful.

John Smith, hanged on December 12, 1705, was cut down after hanging for seven minutes. A reprieve was delivered and his death was no longer necessary or desirable. He was carried to a warm bed for the gory treatment of bloodletting and made a full recovery. "Half-hanged Smith," as he became known, was not a reformed character and found himself before the Old Bailey on at least two further occasions. His ultimate fate is unknown.

In 1728 Margaret Dickson of Musselburgh, Scotland was found guilty of murdering her newborn infant and hanged. Only when friends were carting her body home did she revive. As they approached the coffin, its lid moving slightly. When they opened it she sat upright and they fled in fear.

Defying all odds, William Duell showed no signs of life after being hanged in 1740 until he was transported to the surgeon's table. Only there did an assistant notice he was breathing. The *London Daily Post and General Advertiser* reported: "[he] came so much to himself as to sit up in a chair, groan'd very much and seemed in great agitation but could not speak." When he had recovered his senses Duell said he had been to paradise. Perhaps for the benefit of the law-makers, he said an angel had forgiven him his sins.

THE MAN THEY COULDN'T HANG

Hangman William Calcraft offered his own version of the last gasp to the people of Lancaster, where he carried out executions at the castle. "When you are tied up and your face turned to the Castle wall and the trap falls, you see its stones expanding and contracting violently, and a similar expansion and contraction seems to take place in your own head and breast. Then there is a rush of fire and an earthquake; your eyeballs spring out of their sockets; the castle shoots up in the air and you tumble down a precipice."

Few stories are as haunting as that of John Lee, a murderer who preyed in Babbacombe, southwest England. On February 23, 1885 he stood on the gallows at Exeter prison. Yet when hangman James Berry pulled the lever to open the trap door, nothing happened.

Without the weight of the condemned man, the trapdoor worked perfectly. A second attempt was made, but again the doors would not move. The scene degenerated into farce, with the baffled Berry and colleagues jumping on the trapdoor as Lee stood bound and hooded. Lee was allowed to live, in recognition of the trauma he had suffered. His sentence was commuted to life and he served 22 years before being released.

The next day newspapers told of "The Man They Couldn't Hang." It was an affecting experience for Berry, who had no explanation for the equipment failure, and was later known to seek confessions to soothe his conscience.

In 1945 a former prisoner claimed that the carpenter convict working on the trapdoor instructed Lee to stand on a deliberately warped board to prevent it opening. This supposes Lee had nerves of steel, trusting his fate to the slight movement of one piece of wood!

BELOW: The condemned and their loved ones often prayed for such an incident, but hanging apparatus rarely broke.

HANGING: THE DROP

When a trapdoor was first added to the gallows, the drop did not aid execution as intended. It took the efforts of a diligent hangman to perfect the process.

On May 5, 1760 a mighty throng gathered at Tyburn as a new era beckoned. The victim was Earl Ferrers, the first peer of the realm to be hanged in London, and a new method was on trial.

Ferrers would not be hanged from the horse and cart that conveyed him from his cell at the Tower of London, as felons in the past had been. His death would occur when the floor beneath him gave way, leaving him suspended and strangled. It was known as "the drop."

The momentous event was first spoilt when Earl Ferrers inadvertently broke protocol. He presented the hangman's assistant with five guineas, leaving the empty-handed hangman fuming. Ferrers was forced to wait for his moment of doom while the two officials argued.

Finally, executioner Thomas Turlis was ready to release the mechanism that held the floor in place. Misjudgment by the makers of the scaffold left Ferrers writhing on the rope, with his toes touching the ground. Author Horace Walpole said: "As the machine was new, they were not ready at it; his toes still touched the stage and he suffered a little, having had time, by their bungling to raise his cap; but the executioner pulled it down again and they pulled his legs so that he was soon out of pain and quite dead in four minutes."

Turlis returned to the tried and tested method of horse and cart.

However, the drop was the shape of things to come. It was modified and made an appearance outside Newgate Prison in 1783. Victims were led out from the prison basement directly up the steps and onto the platform, some six feet high.

ABOVE: A man convicted of murdering his mother prepares to be "turned off the ladder," an older, less effective type of hanging.

MARWOOD'S REFINEMENTS

Hangmen still used short ropes which meant that, despite the drop, victims suffered slow strangulation. It wasn't until Lincolnshire man William Marwood took the job of hangman that science was applied. In Ireland there had already been advances in the form of "the long drop." The correct length of rope could be calculated if the prisoner's weight, height, and neck musculature were assessed. With a long drop the neck was broken or dislocated at the end of the fall; death, or at least cessation of pain, was instant.

Marwood drew up a chart to work from, which gave the length of rope necessary for anyone weighing between 112 and 224 pounds. He used a good quality rope—favoring a soft Italian type made of hemp and silk—as it now had to bear not just the weight of the body but the force with which it fell.

Marwood exchanged the traditional slipknot for a metal ring to increase efficiency. He urged the replacement of scaffold ladders with ramps to assist the weak-kneed prisoners on their final walk. Where possible he encouraged the digging of a pit beneath the scaffold, to allow the platform to match the height of the cell floor yet still have the efficient "long drop" beneath it. Marwood's proud boast was that others hanged criminals while he executed them.

He was duly rewarded for his compassion. Unlike his predecessors, Marwood was not abused by street children or reviled by society. His humanity won the respect of everyone from prison governors to his victims.

LEFT: Charles Guiteau, who assassinated America's 20th President, James Garfield, is examined after "the drop" through the scaffold's platform.

SLAVERY

Slavery had existed for centuries. It appears there was no culture, race or creed that was above enslaving neighboring peoples to advance its own ends. However, the Age of Exploration brought fresh impetus to the trade.

ABOVE: One African community preyed on the next, with the European slave traders offering large material incentives.

The pioneering Portuguese began importing slaves from Africa in 1444. Arab traders spread through the continent to exploit the commercial opportunities and thriving slave markets were established in Arabia, Iran, and India. Spain was a major player in the slave trade, along with Britain, France, Denmark, Holland and, later, the American colonies. They used some slaves in their colonies and sold others.

The dangers of disease and other natural hazards kept the Europeans in the African ports, where forts were built to facilitate the trade. They needed go-betweens to breach the interior. Consequently, one African community preyed upon the next to provide the profitable commodity of slaves.

One slave trader described the humiliating process that captured men and women faced at African ports. "[The slaves] are brought out into a large plain, where the surgeons examine every part of every one of them, to the smallest member, men and women being all stark naked. [Rejected slaves are called] Mackrons: being above 35 years of age, or defective in their limbs, eyes or teeth, or grown gray, or have the venereal disease or any other imperfection.... Each of the others, which have passed as good, is marked on the breast, with a red-hot iron, imprinting the mark of the French, English or Dutch companies... care is taken that the women, as tenderest, be not burnt too hard."

Prominent British abolitionist William Wilberforce blamed Britain for the predicament of Africans drawn into slavery. He had grave concerns for the slaves' transportation from Africa to Jamaica or America—the notoriously harsh, grueling Middle Passage.

Long-time opponent of the slave trade William Pitt said that no nation in Europe was "plunged so deeply into this guilt" for slavery as Great Britain. The government, he said, was bound "by the most pressing and indispensable duty" to abolish it.

STOLEN MEN

The Society for the Abolition of the Slave Trade was started in Britain in 1787 by two Anglicans, Granville Sharp and Thomas Clarkson. Quakers and Methodists backed them.

In 1792 Denmark became the first country in Europe to abolish the slave trade. Great Britain legislated against it in 1807 and the United States a year later.

While the human trade was banned there were still slaves until the 1833 Abolition of Slavery Act. French slaves were emancipated in 1848 and Dutch slaves won freedom in 1863.

In America the freedom of slaves became a deeply divisive issue. Slaveholders in the south felt slaves were an essential part of the economy. More industrial states were offended by the continued use of slaves.

As early as 1831 William Lloyd Garrison was threatened with death for his abolitionist view, which he expounded in the newspaper *The Liberator*. "I cannot but regard oppression in every form—and most of all, that which turns a man into a thing—with indignation and abhorrence…. Every slave is a stolen man; every slaveholder is a man stealer."

The American Anti Slavery Society was founded in Philadelphia in 1833 and helped slaves escape to the north. Still, public support was frail until Abraham Lincoln made the abolition of slavery a pillar of his presidential campaign. With the Civil War behind it, slavery was abolished in 1865 by the 13th Amendment.

BELOW: Arabic slave traders drive another convoy of captured men and women toward a market in East Africa.

Slave Punishment

For slaves the torture began when they were torn from their families and taken in fetters hundreds or perhaps thousands of miles to Africa's west coast for sale. But it was far from over.

Slaves were shackled into the hull of a slaver's ship. Kept short of food and water, ventilation, and sanitation, their spirits were quickly eroded. The irons made it virtually impossible to rebel. Famously, the Africans aboard the Spanish slaver *Amistad* overpowered the captain and crew in 1839. Surviving seaman steered them to the United States rather than Africa, where the Africans faced a protracted legal fight before returning home free. However, this kind of occurrence was rare.

Usually slaves remained subjugated. Drawn from tribes across a huge area, they were unlikely to be able to communicate with one another, let alone mount a revolt. Mortality rates among the slaves ran at about 20 percent. The dead were tossed overboard by the crew; those who fell ill might also be thrown into the ocean, to conserve rations.

Slaves were shipped to Brazil by the Portuguese to work on coffee and sugar plantations. They went to other South American destinations to be worked by the Spanish. Many went to the West Indies where, in 1722, a law authorized death for runaway slaves.

Some were taken to Britain. In 1765 Granville Sharp was living with his surgeon brother in London when black man Jonathan Strong appeared. Strong had been pistol-whipped almost to death by his master and then turned onto the streets. Sharp ensured Strong received proper medical care and prevented his owner from taking him back.

CORRECTIVE TREATMENT?

The most sadistic stories of slave punishment came out of North America. Plantation overseers were armed by whips and often accompanied by vicious dogs. They enjoyed legal protection in flogging slaves.

In 1740 an Act of Legislature in America read: "In case any person shall willfully cut out the tongue, put out an eye or cruelly scald, burn, or deprive any slave of any limb or member, or shall inflict any cruel punishment other than by whipping or beating with a horse-whip, cowskin, switch or small-stick, or by putting irons on, or confining or imprisoning such slave, every such person shall for every such offence forfeit the sum of one hundred pounds current money."

It was commonly known that overseers, masters, and even their wives whipped slaves to death. Simon Souther, a plantation owner who whipped and horribly tortured a slave until he died, was sentenced to five years penal servitude in 1851. But convictions like these were few.

Whites used the defense that they were "correcting" errant behavior. Surgeons examining blacks trying to enlist for the Union in the Civil War found one in five bore scars from whipping.

DEMBY'S FATE

A slave, Demby, was being punished by overseer Austin Gore with a whip. Witness Frederick Douglass recalled: "He had given Demby but few stripes, when to get rid of the scourging, he [Demby] plunged himself into a creek and stood there at the depth of his shoulders, refusing to come out. Mr. Gore told him that he would give him three calls, and that… he would shoot him. The first call was given. Demby made no response, but stood his ground. The second and third calls were given with the same result. Mr. Gore then… raised his musket to his face… and in an instant poor Demby was no more. His mangled body sank out of sight and blood and brains marked the water where he had stood." Demby's owner pardoned the overseer.

ARMY DISCIPLINE

Military punishments were merciless. Any rank and file soldier who stepped out of line knew what terrible fate awaited him: a taste of "the cat."

ABOVE: To the left of this picture is a doctor, who can end the punishment if he feels the soldier has taken enough.

The much-feared cat o' nine tails consisted of nine lengths of rope or leather thonging, each measuring at least two feet and knotted in three places. A man flogged by this would have his back, shoulders, and ribs shredded by hundreds of lashes. As the cat's thongs became heavier with blood, their effect worsened. Flogging was authorized in the 1689 Mutiny Act and quickly became a regular feature of army life.

Even minor offenses were resolved by flogging. One soldier received 50 lashes after making a complaint about the quality of bread being served to his regiment. A 60-year-old who had kept an exemplary military record for 30 years was given 300 lashes for one day's absenteeism. Around the same time, a soldier in Gibraltar was flogged to death for being dirty on parade.

Those responsible for whipping—often drum majors—were relieved every 25 strokes, to regain strength. They practiced upon trees, pulping the bark.

John Shipp was one of the soldiers with the duty of flogging. In his book *Flogging and its Substitute* he described its effect: "When the offender was tied, or rather hung up by the hands, his back, from intense cold and the effects of previous floggings, exhibited a complete blue and black appearance. On the first lash the blood spurted out some yards, and, after he had received 50, his back from the neck to the waist, was one continued stream of blood." The victim later committed suicide.

A surgeon was at hand to stop the punishment when the victim was on the brink of his endurance. However, it was difficult to say how much a man could bear before dying. The surgeon's judgment was often awry.

STUNG TO THE HEART

Alexander Somerville, a private in the Scots Guards, described what it was like being whipped: "I felt an astounding sensation between the shoulders under my neck, which went to my toe-nails in one direction, my finger-nails in another, and stung me to the heart as if a knife had gone through my body." He spent eight days in hospital after receiving one hundred lashes.

Greater agonies awaited the men who received the sentence more than once. The pain of newly healed skin being ripped open once again with one stroke was said to be far worse than the numerous strokes of the initial punishment.

Debate over whether flogging was humane or even desirable raged throughout the 19th century. King George III restricted the number of strokes to a thousand in 1807. In 1934 a Royal Commission decided that, while the number of lashes should be lowered further, flogging was a valid punishment. The Duke of Wellington, among others, felt that the threat of a whipping was a deterrent that maintained discipline.

The commission's findings reflected national feelings among civilians, who favored the whip. Sir Robert Peel told the Commons that he "had always been friendly to the punishment of whipping, when exercised within salutary limits… have not been able to find a single instance of abuse for the last seven years."

Clearly he had not been looking at the army and navy, where examples of sadism were not hard to find. The number of lashes was reduced to 50 by the middle of the century and flogging was finally abolished in 1881.

BELOW: There was a scandal in 1903 when a member of the Guards regiment was flogged by fellow officers, years after its abolition.

NAVY DISCIPLINE

Britain had a proud naval heritage. Yet behind the image of the willing, well-drilled sailor in the rigging was a dark side that involved excessive and sadistic discipline.

As early as 1634 the practice of ducking from the yard arm, with the malefactor tied around his middle by a rope, was described in a book: "He is violentlie let fall into the sea, sometimes twise, sometimes three sevrall tymes one after another, and if the offence be very fowle, he is alsoe drawn under the very keele of the shippe, the which is termed keel-rakinge."

A further refinement on the punishment was the firing of a cannon while the victim was underwater, causing him great alarm. Another torturous form of punishment used in the Royal Navy in the 18th century was known as "tying neck and heels." With the victim sitting on the deck, one musket was placed beneath their knees and another behind their neck. The firearms were tied tightly together, exerting such pressure on the body that blood would flow from the nose and ears.

Floggings appears to have been less frequent in the Royal Navy than in the British Army, but more brutal. While their counterparts in the army were expected to stand on one spot, the boatswain's mate, responsible for administering the lash, took a step forward and laid into the stroke.

A CREW'S REVENGE

Sometimes a disgruntled crew exacted revenge on a cruel superior. Hugh Pigot, captain of the *Hermione*, was hacked with cutlasses and thrown overboard. He had ordered floggings of seaman for trivial matters and, when a sailor died during punishment, had the rest of the penalty delivered on his corpse.

RIGHT: Admiral Byng's silk handkerchief drops to the deck as he is shot for cowardice. He took the blame for the failings of the British fleet.

THE NAVY'S SCAPEGOAT

After each stroke the mate separated the thonging with his fingers, to cause maximum discomfort on the next lash. One 19th century observer wrote:" 'Tis a severe punishment thus; and I do not think any man could stand nine dozen as I have seen it 'laid in'." In 1801 a naval lieutenant was brought to trial after three seamen were flogged to death in Bombay without a prior court martial. Floggings carried out in tropical countries left the victim vulnerable to infection and fever and almost always resulted in death.

The worst offense aboard ship was cowardice in the face of enemy action; the punishment was death. Admiral John Byng faced this charge following his withdrawal from Minorca in 1756, leaving the English defenders of the island at the mercy of the French. Byng was guilty of defeatism rather than cowardice—he knew his veteran ships faced a mauling from the French. However, the government wished to obliterate the military reversals it had suffered by use of a scapegoat. General William Blakeney, the man forced to surrender Minorca, was quick to blame Byng for the misfortune. Byng was found guilty of "not doing his utmost to take or destroy the enemy's ships." On March 14, 1757 he was led to the quarterdeck of the *Monarque* where, knelt on a cushion with a handkerchief over his eyes, he was shot.

When the Army Act of 1881 curtailed the flogging of soldiers, the British Navy acted to stop it occurring aboard ship. Nevertheless, young soldiers and sailors were still liable to be birched. Corporal punishment in the United States Navy, however, was abolished in 1850.

ABOVE: A midshipman faces a naval examination board, having already been ducked into the sea as a punishment.

FORERUNNERS OF THE GUILLOTINE

The low thunder of the guillotine blade dropping was the last earthly sound heard by thousands of victims in France. Contrary to popular belief, this cold, quick method of execution was pioneered elsewhere.

Although Dr. Joseph Guillotin has lent his name to the plummeting sheet-blade, it was probably invented in a simpler form by a Roman in the days of the Empire. It is thought that such a device dispatched one of the Apostles, former tax collector St. Matthew.

Persians of the 10th century mimicked the contraption, using a hefty mallet to send the blade on its way. In 1307 a similar machine executed Murcod Ballagh at Merton, Ireland. It reappeared in Britain, perhaps as early as 1286, in Halifax, where it was in use until 1654. Parish records from 1541 reveal that more than 50 people died before it was scrapped.

Its blade, which resembles an ax head, has been preserved, however. It weighs 7lb 12oz, measures 10 inches in length, and was held aloft by a wedge or pin. A description of the "Halifax Gibbet" was published in 1587.

"The engine wherewith the execution is done is a square block of wood, of the length of four-and-a-half feet which doth ride up and down in a slot between two pieces of timber that are framed and set upright, of five yards in height. In the lower end of the sliding block is a blade keyed or fastened into the wood which, being drawn up into the frame, is there fastened by a wooden pin.

LIVESTOCK BECOMES EXECUTIONER

"In the middle of the pin is a long rope fastened, that cometh down among the people, so that when the offender has made his confession and hath laid his neck over the base block, every man there doth either take hold of the rope, or putteth forth his arm as near to the rope as he can, in token that he is willing to see justice done. Pulling out the pin in this manner, the block wherein the blade is fastened doth fall down with such a violence that even if the neck of the transgressor be as thick as a bull, it would still be cut asunder at a stroke, and roll from the body by a huge distance."

If the victim was convicted of rustling sheep, the rope that operated the blade was attached to such an animal and it was driven forward to release the pin. This was a typical medieval notion of justice. The last two victims of the Halifax Gibbet were guilty of stealing two horses and 30 yards of cloth.

James Douglas, Earl of Morton, was so impressed with Halifax's "guillotine" that he commissioned one for use in Edinburgh, christened the Scottish Maiden. Built in 1564, the iron and steel blade held within a stout oak frame was weighted with lead, bringing it up to a hefty 75 pounds.

Ironically, the Earl gained first-hand experience of the brutal efficiency of the Maiden after he was accused of complicity in the murder of Darnley, husband of Mary, Queen of Scots. He laid before the Maiden in 1581 and his severed head was displayed on a pike.

The last victim of the Scottish Maiden was the Earl of Argyll, one of the Rye House plotters who tried to kill King Charles II and his brother James in 1683. It then stood unused for decades before it was dismantled in 1710.

ABOVE: The "guillotine" used in Merton, Ireland, was the ancestor of the Halifax Gibbet, Scottish Maiden, and the relatively sophisticated device used during the French Revolution.

LEFT: A horse is being driven forward to pull the holding pin clear of the Halifax Gibbet, releasing a 10-inch blade that could slice through the strongest of necks.

129

THE GUILLOTINE'S INNOVATORS

The man credited with launching France's famous decapitation machine was Dr. Guillotin. Bizarrely, his motives were humanitarian and his empathy with convicted prisoners sincere.

ABOVE: Dr. Joseph Guillotin argued for an efficient execution method, used regardless of the convict's social standing.

RIGHT: The guillotine used to kill a king. Executed in 1793, Louis XVI reputedly assisted in its design.

On October 10, 1789 Dr. Joseph Ignace Guillotin argued in front of the newly formed French Assembly. He called for the same method of execution to apply to rich and poor, and for it to be delivered in a uniform manner, by machine, to rule out human vagaries. Further, Guillotin wanted the estates of the condemned left untouched by the state, their families to be protected from public abuse, and for the bodies of the executed to be returned to their loved ones for burial.

Within two years the French deputies, won over by his arguments, declared that "every person condemned to the death penalty shall have his head severed." Advice was sought. What method would satisfy Guillotin's desire for a quick, dignified method of dispatch?

Dr. Antoine Louis from the Academy of Surgery urged Guillotin to investigate the Halifax Gibbet and the Scottish Maiden. "This apparatus would not be felt and would hardly be perceptible," he insisted. The evidence was persuasive. In the spring of 1792 German harpsichord maker Tobias Schmidt was paid 960 francs to build an imitation of the British models. Although similar to its cross-Channel cousins, the French version was refined with a hinged bench (a *bascule*), upon which the condemned were strapped and swung into position. Victims no longer had to kneel in position; they were supported in their final moments, reducing the margin of error.

TOO EFFICIENT?

Within a month it was tested on human corpses to monitor its efficacy, then on live animals. It is said that King Louis XVI, visiting Schmidt in disguise, suggested that the curved blade be changed for one with an oblique angle, to improve efficiency.

On April 25, 1792 the guillotine went into action for the first time in Paris. The victim was highwayman Nicholas-Jacques Pelletier, but while executioner Charles-Henri Sanson was impressed with his new machine, the crowds departed in disappointment. It was over too quickly and lacked the drama of hangings and the like.

The contraption was first called the Louisette, after Dr. Louis, but the name was dropped in favor of others, including the National Razor, the Widow, the People's Avenger, and the Red Theatre. However, it was "guillotine," inspired by the man who shook up the capital punishment system, that stuck.

Already the French Revolution was underway. The king had been mobbed at Versailles in 1789, the Bastille was stormed, and the new Assembly had made a Declaration of the Rights of Man. But when the guillotine made its debut, the appalling butchery that lay ahead was largely unsuspected.

THE RELUCTANT EXECUTIONER

The man who first operated the guillotine, Charles-Henri Sanson, was one of a dynasty in charge of capital punishment in Paris. He became deputy to his father, Jean Baptiste, at the age of 15 and continued working into old age. Charles-Henri was smartly dressed, musically talented, and literate. He drew no pleasure from the sufferings of those he dispatched, working throughout the Reign of Terror efficiently but not enthusiastically, realizing that if he refused to do the job his own head would be on the block. His lowest moment on the scaffold was seeing his son Gabriel perish in 1792, after slipping in a pool of blood and tumbling from the guillotine platform. Afterward he insisted that platforms were ringed by railings.

GUILLOTINE IN OVERDRIVE

When Queen Marie Antoinette was told the French peasants had no bread, she supposedly said, "Let them eat cake." The remark was taken as typical of an isolated monarchy out of touch with its people, and revolution was a step closer.

ABOVE: The birth charts of Louis XVI and Marie Antoinette, illustrated with their executions on January 21 and October 16, 1793, respectively.

RIGHT: In this satirical etching from 1793 the French Revolutionary Robespierre has run out of victims and resorts to guillotining the executioner.

The saying "Let them eat cake" was well known in France years before Marie Antoinette arrived from her native Austria. Philosopher Jean Jacques Rousseau, an unwitting architect of the French Revolution through his "Social Contract" of 1762, believed it a cliché.

But there is no doubt that by the end of the 18th century France was burdened with an outdated feudal system. Taxes levied to pay for four costly wars in the half-century before 1783 crippled rural aristocrats and the middle classes. The peasants struggled through a series of hard winters and poor harvests, and the urban poor spent the majority of their wages on bread.

Louis XVI sensed that the tide was turning against the monarchy and the government was called together in 1789 (the first time since 1614). Traditionally, the government comprised of three sections: the clergy, the nobility, and the commons. Now the commons took the initiative and declared itself a national assembly. Soon afterward an angry mob stormed the Bastille in a symbolic gesture—it housed only nine prisoners—and a new order became inevitable.

Initially moderates tried to govern with a monarchy in place, but the over-riding mood was unforgiving. In 1791 the king and his wife left Paris for only the second time in his reign, but they were stopped at Varennes and escorted back to Paris.

THE CRIME OF ARISTOCRACY

By April 1792 war broke out between Austria and France. Worsening tensions led to an uprising by extremists in the summer. The French National Convention now running the country turned its attentions to Louis XVI. In a powerful speech before the Convention, journalist Camille Desmoulins assured his listeners, "It is a crime to be a king."

The execution of Louis XVI in January 1793 was intended to heal the country's wounds and close the sorry chapter. Alas, this was not to be. In April 1793 the radical Committee of Public Safety was formed, charged with securing the position of the new France. Its instant remedy was to rid the country of the enemies within. The Terror began.

An uprising that had won support from across the classes suddenly became a bitter class war. Anyone who was an aristocrat was sent to the guillotine. As the state-sponsored violence escalated, chief executioner Charles-Henri Sanson and his men guillotined 300 men and women in three days. Between April 6, 1793 and July 29, 1795 almost 3,000 were executed.

Among the victims was Marie Antoinette, who so feared for her safety that her hair had turned gray. Committed revolutionary Charlotte Corday was nevertheless

sickened by the violence and in a bid to halt the excesses murdered Jean-Paul Marat, a leading revolutionary who had suggested that he become dictator of France. After her execution Sanson's assistant François le Gros lifted her head and slapped her cheek. Sanson was furious and had le Gros imprisoned for three months.

Jeanne du Barry, former mistress of Louis XVI and an acquaintance of Sanson in his youth, went kicking and screaming to her death. Lawyer Maximilien de Robespierre, who fostered a personality cult and wielded supreme power on the Committee, was denounced and guillotined in 1794.

The river of blood at last dried to a trickle. The people were undoubtedly relieved, although statesman Charles-Maurice de Talleyrand used another well-worn phrase to sum up their response: "They have learnt nothing and forgotten nothing."

THE 20TH CENTURY

The 20th century saw the advent of the United Nations and the human rights watchdog Amnesty International. Technological leaps made communication and travel easier than ever. Political barriers were thrown up—then torn down. All the evidence pointed to a new, enlightened age.

Alas, execution and torture were not consigned to history. Indeed, those in favor of the death penalty became increasingly entrenched. Human rights remained subject to appalling abuses. In the new millennium things seem set to change.

Since 1985 more than 35 countries have scrapped capital punishment or restricted its application. Only four countries that abolished the death penalty have re-introduced it. One, Nepal, had yet another change of heart and banned it.

Some have bowed to political pressure. In order to join the Council of Europe, a country must ban the death penalty. Desire to become part of the council has led to the Ukraine and Georgia stopping executions; death row prisoners have had their punishments commuted to life. In one of his last acts as President, Boris Yeltsin commuted the death sentence for all 716 prisoners on Russia's death row.

For some, the fresh approach appears to have its roots in a genuine desire to cast off the shackles of the past and move forward into a new era. Public opinion, particularly in America, where support for the death penalty has been traditionally strong, appears to be mollifying.

Illustrating the cross-cultural nature of the issue, the President of Malawi has recently declared he would never sign a death warrant: "Life is sacred. It is only for God to take, not for me." And when Turkmenistan abolished the death penalty, President Saparmurat Niyaz stated, "Now in our country, neither the government nor anyone else has the right to take away human life."

RIGHT: The search for a clean, efficient, painless method of execution has occupied those in favor of capital punishment in the second half of the 20th Century. The electric chair became the symbol of execution, as the guillotine had been before it, but many believe that death is not a just form of retribution.

EXECUTION IN THE 21ST CENTURY

Few debates attract the same kind of vehemence as those concerning capital punishment. Are the simple motives of justice and retribution enough to justify a pre-meditated killing?

Certain crimes appear so appalling that capital punishment seems the appropriate response. It is the only way society can be sure that such offences will not be repeated. Once the prisoner is executed, the state saves money in terms of food and guardianship.

The families of the raped or murdered sometimes have their pain eased by the death of an assailant. The penalty may deter others from committing a similar heinous deed.

For those who oppose execution, a murder is a murder. State-sponsored killing is no better than death at the hands of a common criminal. It is perhaps worse, for it is pre-meditated and cold-blooded.

Amnesty International campaigns tirelessly for the abolition of the death penalty. It declares that people have a basic right to life—according to the Universal Declaration of Human Rights, proclaimed by the General Assembly of the United Nations in 1948. This is a fundamental right that cannot be withdrawn by way of punishment.

The death penalty is retained in a number of countries that criticize the cruelty of torture. Yet for a prisoner to know the date of his or her own death is a heavy burden indeed. Some of the condemned in America are even asked to choose their means of execution.

Numerous statistics have been compiled on the topic, some validating the deterrent effect of the death penalty, others claiming there is none. It seems the latter are in the majority: Comparisons have been drawn between US states which retain the death penalty and neighboring states that do not. Time and again, it appears states with capital punishment have higher murder rates. Some figures indicate that murders increase following an execution, the theory being that society in general and criminals in particular are brutalized by it. The official line of the United Nations is that "The evidence as a whole still gives no positive support to the deterrent hypothesis."

FLAWS OF THE SYSTEM

American states that support the death penalty are in the minority in the modern West. Countries like Italy are so adamantly opposed to it that they refuse to allow the extradition of suspects if they are in danger of facing capital punishment.

Opponents are concerned about the seemingly random element of the death penalty. In one year alone there were 22,000 killings in America, while just 300 people were sentenced to death.

Most persuasive of all arguments against capital punishment is the death of an innocent man. It is estimated that at least 400 innocent people were convicted of capital crimes in America during the 20th century. Of those, 23 were executed.

Figures prove that it is more costly to pursue a death penalty case through the courts, with its appeals and publicity, than it is to keep that prisoner behind bars for his or her lifetime. In court there are jurors who are reluctant to convict if they know it will mean the death of the prisoner.

It is impossible to generalize about the emotions of the close family of a killer's victim. Some are troubled by the death of the felon. Before Karla Faye Tucker was executed in 1998, close relatives of the people she killed pleaded for her life to be spared.

In 1998 there were 2,258 known executions in 37 countries, with the most occurring in China, Iran, the Democratic Republic of Congo, and the United States. By the year 2000, 106 countries worldwide had abolished the death penalty, in practice or in law; 90 countries retain it.

Above: People protested against the death penalty when Gary Graham received his sentence for murdering Bobby Lambert in a Texas grocery store parking lot, to no avail. There was little evidence and only one of eight witnesses identified Graham as the gunman, but he was executed by lethal injection on June 22, 2000.

LAST DAYS OF THE GUILLOTINE

The stark silhouette of the guillotine loomed large in the minds of the French. It became ingrained in their culture, and the blade's use was not abolished till 1981.

At the height of the Terror of the French Revolution, cart after cart unloaded miserable guillotine fodder, the majority meeting death with discipline and dignity. Perhaps it was these qualities of self-control that permitted the public to withstand so many deaths.

Charles-Henri Sanson and his men prided themselves on the speed at which they could secure victims to the *bascule* bench and swing it into position. On one day Sanson claimed to have executed 22 people within 36 minutes.

Virtually no one fought, kicked, or abused in their final moments. The passive acceptance of the victims appeared to infect the mob. Some women were so accepting of the bloody spectacle that they knitted as they watched.

The image of the guillotine was used to decorate plates, cups. and snuffboxes. Miniature guillotines were produced as cigar cutters and even as children's toys. Death masks of victims were made into a popular attraction by Dr. Philippe Curtius and Marie Grosholtz, better known as Madame Tussaud. The artistic Marie was given access to the severed heads of all the famous guillotine victims, including the royals, Robespierre, and the well-known revolutionaries who went under the blade. After moving to Britain, Marie made death masks of notorious villains.

CONSCIOUSNESS DRAINS

The guillotine remained in use across France after the revolution. Every city had its guillotine and usually boasted a famous family of executioners.

The last public execution took place in 1939 at Versailles; murderer Eugene Weidmann was the victim. Although the hour was early, in a bid to deter crowds, a great number attended. The government instantly legislated against public execution, and war criminals tried and convicted were guillotined behind closed doors. The guillotine was used for the last time on September 10, 1977 and finally outlawed in 1981.

Public curiosity about the guillotine has barely faded. One of the key questions that has perplexed people over the centuries is whether the severed head can remain responsive. Various experiments have

MLLE. MARCHADIER

MME. JAUME

MLLE. BABELAY

MME. COLOMB

MME. CRUCHET

MME. LABORDE LINE

LANDRU'S

GARDEN

MME. GUILLIN

MME. BUISSON.

BLUEBEARD.

MME. PASCAL

been carried out, most of which point to some level of consciousness in the first seconds after the blade falls.

After a criminal called Languille was guillotined in the early hours of June 29, 1905, one Dr. Beaurieux conducted some basic experiments. He noticed the eyes and lips contracting for a few seconds before the facial expression of the dead man relaxed. After waiting a few seconds more, Beaurieux called out "Languille." He saw the eyes slowly lift up and focus on his own. Languille's eyes closed until his name was repeated, some seconds later. "The eyelids lifted and undeniably living eyes fixed themselves on mine with perhaps even more penetration than the first time." After 30 seconds had elapsed, there was no further response.

ABOVE: Henri "Bluebeard" Landru attracted women using "lonely hearts" advertisements, gained their confidence, and murdered them for their riches. He went to the guillotine in 1922.

LEFT: This reconstruction shows Madame Tussaud producing the death mask of Marie Antoinette.

ELECTRIC CHAIR

When convicted killer Pedro Medina was executed in Florida's electric chair in 1997, flames leapt from the helmet covering his head. The death penalty debate moved center-stage once more.

RIGHT: The electric chair—also known as "Sparky," "Old Smokey" and "The Hot Squat"—is now giving way to lethal injection. In 1985 Justice William P. Brennan revealed, "When the post-electrocution autopsy is performed the liver is so hot that doctors say it cannot be touched by the human hand."

BELOW: Thomas Alva Edison, inventor of the light bulb, was reluctantly drawn into the death by electrocution debate. He acted to maintain the public's trust in direct current electricity.

The electric chair was first used in New York on August 6, 1890, to dispatch wife-killer William Kemmler. Its design owes much to Thomas Edison (1847–1931), the pioneer of electricity. He opposed capital punishment but operated "behind the scenes" to ensure the use of alternating current, rival to his direct current, thereby discrediting AC electricity by its association with death.

A charge of 1,300 volts for 17 seconds failed to kill Kemmler; his life was taken with a further shock that lasted more than one minute. Witnesses were concerned that death was so long coming. The *New York Times* called the chair "a disgrace to civilization." George Westinghouse, who developed alternating current and spent considerable effort trying to save Kemmler from the chair, said "They would have done better with an axe!"

Other American states chose to follow the New York example and various designers and makers from across America earned the dubious accolade of "father of the electric chair." Fundamentally, the condemned is strapped into the chair, which is usually made of oak, and saline-soaked, sponge-tipped electrodes are attached to their ankles and shaved head, by way of a helmet. The executioner administers a shock of about 2,000 volts for a minute or more to render the condemned unconscious, followed by two smaller charges, then a further full shock.

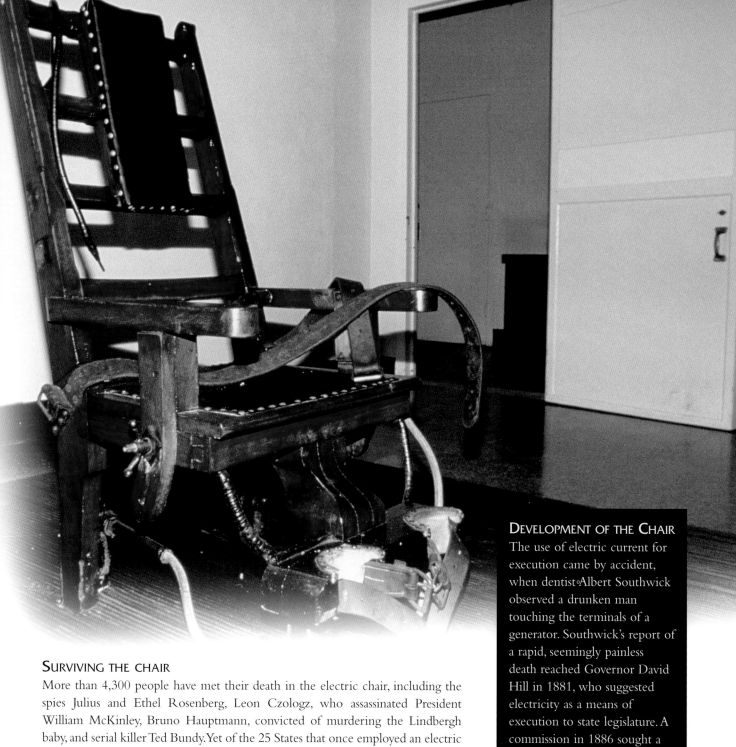

SURVIVING THE CHAIR

More than 4,300 people have met their death in the electric chair, including the spies Julius and Ethel Rosenberg, Leon Czologz, who assassinated President William McKinley, Bruno Hauptmann, convicted of murdering the Lindbergh baby, and serial killer Ted Bundy. Yet of the 25 States that once employed an electric chair, only four have retained its services: Florida, Georgia, Alabama, and Nebraska.

Its diminishing popularity is linked with the horror stories that surround it. Medina's fiery end was by no means unique. Flames and smoke came from the hood worn by policeman-killer Jesse Taferno in 1990; it took the warders over four minutes to deliver a charge sufficient to knock him out. It took five jolts and 17 minutes for William Vandiver to die in Indiana, 1985.

Many chairs were antiques before they were abandoned. Following the outcry over Medina, Florida invested in a new model, only to have its first occupant—murderer Allen Lee Davis in July 1999—bleed profusely from the chest and mouth.

Cables were incorrectly connected to Willie Francis, allegedly by drunken staff. The voltage was insufficient to kill him on May 3, 1946. A subsequent appeal to the US Supreme Court failed and he was returned to the chair the following year. This time it was in full working order.

DEVELOPMENT OF THE CHAIR

The use of electric current for execution came by accident, when dentist Albert Southwick observed a drunken man touching the terminals of a generator. Southwick's report of a rapid, seemingly painless death reached Governor David Hill in 1881, who suggested electricity as a means of execution to state legislature. A commission in 1886 sought a humane method of execution, and two years later electrocution became New York's capital punishment. Under the direction of The Medico-Legal Society, inventor Harold Brown and Dr. Fred Peterson experimented on animals for six months, using varying quantities of alternating and direct current. On January 1, 1889, the Electric Execution Law came into effect.

GAS CHAMBER

While prisoners in a gas chamber are rendered unconscious within seconds, it can take up to 18 minutes for the body to give up its fight for life. Despite modifications, the gas chamber has few supporters.

The suffering endured by pigs in the first, prototype gas chamber appalled journalists. Unlike electrocution, gas does not paralyze, so the agonized writhings of victims are disturbingly apparent.

Nevertheless, Nevada adopted the gas chamber as a means of execution in 1921. Three years later, Jon Gee was the first man to die in it. It was first used in North Carolina in 1936, when a local reporter, a veteran of some 156 electrocutions, told how he witnessed "awful butchery." Its opponents were largely ignored: By 1973, 13 states had gas chambers.

Its design and operation have been improved. The steel chamber is furnished with a single chair—in North Carolina it is the state's old electric chair. Straps keep the limbs in place and the condemned wears a mask with a nose hole.

From outside the hermetically sealed chamber, warders operate a mechanism that mixes hydrochloric acid and potassium cyanide in a pan within, forming the fatal hydrocyanic gas. They have the security of knowing that cyanide detectors sound an alarm if the gas leaks. For a fleeting moment the prisoner may see the fumes, before he feels its effects following inhalation.

Double-paned glass allows those in the witness chamber to see the prisoner's death throes. There are even beakers of sulfuric acid between the two panes to prevent condensation.

Death occurs quickly for the prisoner who breathes normally. Those who hold their breath by way of natural response to the gas suffer a more lingering demise. A heart monitor attached to the condemned reveals when his life ends.

A CALL TOO LATE

The deadly gas is cleared with carbon filters or ammonia before prison warders enter the room. Even so, the first to enter some 30 minutes after executions wear a gas mask. They decontaminate the body with bleach to prevent harm coming to anyone who touches it—specifically the undertaker.

Gas chambers have become increasingly unpopular. In California, for example, gas was outlawed as unconstitutional in 1994. While technically remaining an option in six American states, it is likely to be used in just two.

Among those killed in the gas chambers were Barbara Graham, whose execution in 1955 was halted twice in the same day—once at the chamber door. Caryl Chessman—the "Red Light Bandit" who preyed on women in Hollywood—was convicted in 1948.

Chessman was a reformed character by the time of his death in San Quentin, 1960. He had become a student of philosophy and law—in a bid to save his life—and wrote several books.

He saw himself fighting "a dogged and seemingly endless battle for survival, of watching nearly five dozen men take that fast grim walk past my cell." It was "an incredible, nightmarish experience."

MARTYRS TO EXECUTION

At least two prisoners in North Carolina in the 1990s chose to die by gas because they thought they would suffer more, arousing ire among local politicians. One Republican who favored a ban on gas in favor of lethal injection said: "It's primarily a safety issue.... Some inmates have used [execution by gas chamber] to make a statement or 'showboat'."

Chessman's nightmare was not over. Moments after the deadly gas was released, a phone call confirmed another stay of execution. The wardens thought it too late to save him and the execution continued as planned. Chessman died although the judiciary thought he should live; he was both defeated and triumphant.

ABOVE: The gas chamber has been used in up to 13 American states since 1924, but its popularity has waned.

LETHAL INJECTION

The first to die from lethal injection was Charlie Brooks in Texas, 1982, but it was initially considered for a means of execution in 1888. It remains popular, and was introduced in Guatemala as recently as 1998.

Clean and quiet, lethal injection is the most favored method of execution in the USA. Some 35 states have used it above alternatives since 1977 and it has dispatched more than 460 prisoners.

The prisoner is rigged up to two drips through which he or she is fed sodium thiopental, which induces sleep; the muscle-relaxant pancuronium bromide, which paralyses the lungs; and finally potassium chloride, to stop the heart.

It seems it remarkably sanitary way to die, with no one getting their hands dirty. The prisoner falls asleep, like some improbable Aurora, but there is no miraculous awakening. If the drugs cocktail is inexpertly mixed, however, the prisoner may be trapped in the terrifying limbo of paralysis before death occurs.

It isn't always easy to administer. Given that many prisoners on death row have been intravenous drug users, it can be difficult to find a vein that won't collapse when the necessary drips are attached. Arkansas killer Ricky Ray Rector was kept waiting for 45 minutes as medics struggled to insert the tubes. Ultimately, Rector himself lent a hand.

Some are in favor of the death penalty but opposed to lethal injection, as they believe perpetrators of capital crimes should not be spared from suffering. By fading away in an apparently peaceable manner, the deterrent factor is not emphasized.

A QUIET DEATH

Those against state-sponsored killings are concerned that lethal injection attracts little publicity. High-profile executions and the media circus that surrounds them are likely to wear down public tolerance for capital punishment. The softly-softly nature of lethal injections keeps their news value to little more than a paragraph. As Democrat Senator Frank W. Balance put it, "The man is just as dead if you hang him, shoot him or cut his head off. The easier you make it to kill people the less attention people will pay to it and the longer it will go on."

Prisoners still have to endure the torturous wait for the appointed day of death and undergo the terror of being strapped at the legs and arms onto a trolley. The process does not take place in the caring atmosphere of a hospital, but the harsh surroundings of a prison.

The end isn't always peaceful: When Joseph Cannon was executed on April 22, 1998 in Huntsville, Texas, the needle blew out of his arm at the moment the fatal drugs began to flow. Cannon was convicted of killing his sister Anne Walsh just as the USA resumed executions in 1977, when he was 17 years old. He was hit by a truck at the age of four and suffered a fractured skull. His life, shadowed by brain damage and abuse, came to an end after 21 years on death row, during which he learned to read and write.

Like Cannon, Robert Carter was 17 when he committed murder, shooting Sylvia Reyes. He too was brain-damaged, with a low IQ, and had suffered brutal abuse as a child. It took a jury just 10 minutes to find him guilty. Carter was on death row for 16 years. The prison chaplain, with Carter during his last hours, said later, "Robert was very calm, very peaceful. He was very polite and very gentle. He'd changed a lot. He was a man truly filled with remorse for what had taken place."

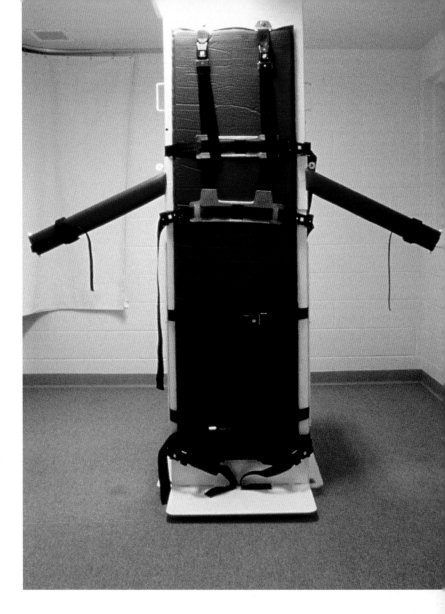

ABOVE: Death by lethal injection appears to be a comfortable way to die. As such it fails to satisfy the pro-death penalty lobby, which sees it as a soft option for killers.

LEFT: In 1984 James Autry was killed by lethal injection. An observer said the condemned took more than ten minutes to die and was conscious and in pain.

145

FIRING SQUAD

Firing squads were widely used in Mexico during the years of civil unrest at the start of the century. They have been used in countries such as England, the USA, and Cuba, and are still employed today.

On January 17, 1977 a firing squad was ready to end the ten-year moratorium that prevented capital punishment in the USA. "Let's do it," said Gary Gilmore, after a target was pinned over his heart. He was led out before marksmen in the warehouse at Utah State prison. Four shots felled Gilmore, who had killed two students at Brigham Young University the previous year.

The death penalty had been put on hold in 1967 in response to widespread public distaste for state-sponsored violence, in the wake of the Vietnam War. Death rows everywhere were emptied as capital penalties were replaced with life or long-term prison sentences. However, key legal hearings during the ensuing decade opened the door for its re-introduction.

In the USA, where policies on such crucial issues are determined at state level, a bevy of commissions were established to scrutinize the case for capital punishment. Highly-focused bills eased discretionary execution back onto the agenda in 35 states by 1976.

Gary Gilmore was the first to die under those new laws, having chosen not to challenge his sentence. He was one of only two people to be killed by firing squad since the modern era of capital punishments in America began. Both shootings took place in Utah.

Most members of firing squads are ordered to aim for the large, easy target of the torso, rather than the head. Bullet wounds to the body do not always kill efficiently and the prisoner can take many minutes to die.

It is common practice to issue blanks to one or more of the men responsible for pulling the trigger without their knowledge, so they are saved from feelings of remorse.

CASTRO'S METHOD

A report by a British Royal Commission into capital punishment in 1953 concluded that the firing squad was a poor form of execution. "It does not possess even the first requisite of an efficient method; the certainty of causing immediate death." Britain had employed firing squads to kill 15 Irish nationalists during the Easter Rising of 1916 and those found guilty of espionage during the First World War. Most shootings took place at the Tower of London.

But far from being consigned to history, firing squads are in use today in countries across the world. Brutal dictator Nicolae Ceausescu and his wife Elena were shot on Christmas Day in 1989 after being found guilty of crimes against the Rumanian people.

Castro favors the firing squad in Cuba, where the number of deaths through capital punishment rose sharply at the end of the millennium, corresponding with a hike in crime rates. Under Cuban law there are 112 crimes that now attract the death penalty, including cattle rustling.

In Palestine firing squads are used to kill convicted criminals, who are usually blindfolded and tied to a pole before the shooting starts. In Sierra Leone 24 army officers were similarly executed by Nigerians who intervened following a coup in 1998.

Two men convicted of raping and killing a young boy were whipped, shot, and then strung up in southern Yemen as recently as 1999. As is common in the area, hundreds of people watched the execution, and the bodies were left on view for three days to deter further violent crime.

ABOVE: Gary Gilmore's death ushered in a new era in America, following ten years without capital punishment. Gilmore donated his eyes for scientific research.

LEFT: A traitor shot near a railway track in France, 1914. English and French soldiers in the First World War were shot for cowardice.

HANGING AND THE JUDICIAL SYSTEM

The case against mother of two Ruth Ellis was straightforward: her trial took two days and the jury found her guilty within half an hour. When she was sentenced to hang, she showed no emotion. Yet Ellis became a symbol of rough justice.

Ruth Ellis shot her lover David Blakely in cold blood on Easter Sunday 1955. But there was something about this platinum-haired former model and her crime of passion that touched the souls of many. Ellis's background had been troubled, with one failed marriage already behind her. True, she was consumed with a passionate jealousy for Blakely and tormented him with accusations of infidelity, but in return he was violent and crudely insensitive.

THE HANGMAN'S POST
In 1999 Maweni Simelane, Minister of Justice in Swaziland, was overwhelmed with eager hopefuls when he appealed for a new national hangman. The successful applicant was not likely to be overworked. Although there are eight people on death row, the last execution occurred in 1983.

Blakely's death occurred two weeks after Ellis suffered a miscarriage induced by his physical abuse. She snapped after seeing him flirting with another woman. In a different generation, Ellis would be seen as a woman who deserved compassion and help, rather than the rope.

Her death at Holloway Women's Prison, London, on July 13, 1955 did much to hasten reform of the laws in England. She was the last woman in the country to be executed; the death penalty was finally outlawed in 1965.

Other controversies in England furthered the cause of abolitionists. Derek Bentley, 19, was hanged at Wandsworth jail on January 28, 1953 for the shooting and death of a policeman. However, it was acknowledged that his accomplice, Christopher Craig, had pulled the trigger. At 16 Craig was too young to hang and was jailed instead.

The pair were attempting to rob a warehouse in Croydon, London, when they were surrounded by police. The jury heard how Bentley cried out: "Let him have it, Chris." They decided he encouraged Craig to fire. But Bentley's defense and family maintained the doomed young man was urging his cohort to hand over the gun, in response to a request by the police. A plea for clemency by 200 Members of Parliament failed to stop the execution.

ABOVE: Albert Pierrepoint was the hangman at the Ellis execution. Although he had a long career as an executioner, he became an opponent of the death penalty.

A FALLIBLE SYSTEM

In February 1998 an appeal court overturned the conviction of Mahmood Hussein Mattan, a Somali hung in September 1952, after finding evidence of racism at the trial. The judge commented, "Capital punishment was not a prudent culmination for the criminal justice system which is human and therefore fallible."

However, British resolve to stop hanging was sorely tested with the trial of child killers Ian Brady and Myra Hindley. Between their arrest in October 1965 and conviction in May 1966, the death penalty was abolished. Evidence of the cruelty that both displayed to their young victims appalled the nation and led to calls for its return.

Much later, Hindley admitted that hanging might have been appropriate. "I knew I was a selfish coward but I couldn't bear the thought of being hung, although… it would have solved so many problems. The family of the victims would have derived some peace of mind and the tabloids would not have been able to exploit and manipulate them as they do to this day. My own family, although they would have been devastated at my being hung and the reasons why, would have come to terms with it."

Hanging is one of the options open to death row prisoners in two American states, but since 1976 only three people have chosen hanging above lethal injection.

LEFT: Glamorous Ruth Ellis sought the ultimate revenge. Yet many doubted the wisdom of her execution; thousands gathered outside Holloway Prison on the morning of her hanging.

DEATH ROW, USA

Thousands of men spend years on death row, watching helplessly as fellow inmates are led to their execution. Although the execution rate seems to be increasing, the empty ranks are quickly filled.

BELOW: Hoyt Clines, 37, was executed in the first triple execution in 32 years in Arkansas.

Inside the prison a man prepares to die for a crime committed years before. At the gates are two opposing groups: One believes justice is being done, the other is adamantly opposed to the death penalty. Often they clash, both sides claiming greater grief and the moral high ground. The vigil ends when a guard comes to the gate to announce the deed is done.

Death row has lost an inmate. His passing has a profound effect on those left behind. It is part of the punishment process; men must confront numerous other deaths before facing their own.

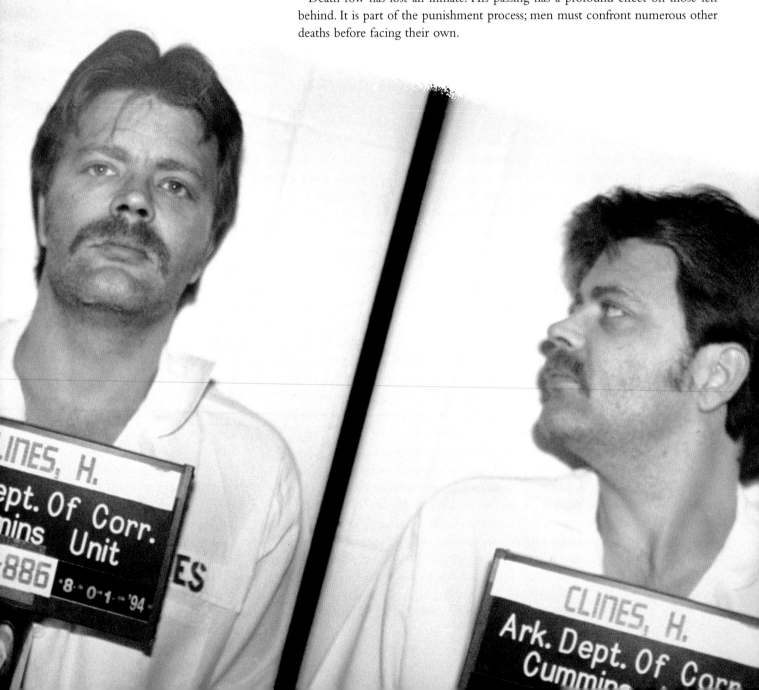

CLINES, H.
ept. Of Corr.
mins Unit
886 ·8·0·1·'94

CLINES, H.
Ark. Dept. Of Corr
Cummin

There are more than 3,600 men on death row in the USA. California has the highest death row population (551 in 1999), followed by Texas—which also has the highest number of annual executions. There were 98 executions in America in 1999, the most since 1976.

In 1994 President Bill Clinton signed an Act that expanded the types of crime punishable by the federal death penalty. Opponents point to numerous hurdles that might hinder the accused.

They might have been poorly advised by an inexperienced court-appointed attorney. Those destined for death row are usually poor and often illiterate.

They might have been the victims of prejudice. Time and again, racial overtones have been detected in capital cases. While black and Latino people comprise less than a quarter of America's population, they represent nearly half of the prisoners on death row.

They might be brain-damaged or otherwise mentally deficient. In 1989 the Supreme Court decided that it is not a violation of the Eighth Amendment to execute people who are retarded.

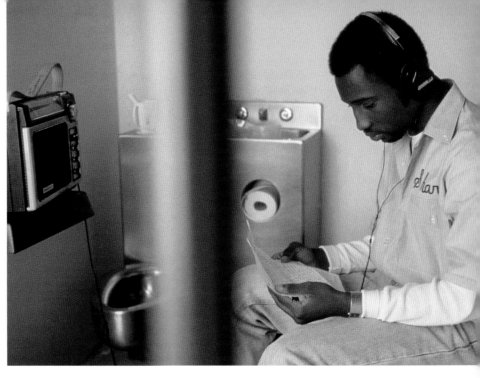

ABOVE: Shareef Cousin, 19, in Louisiana, is one of numerous teenagers on death row. They derive cold comfort from the knowledge that America is one of only six countries to have executed youths who were under the age of 18 when they committed a capital offense.

YOUTH AND INNOCENCE

One in 50 is likely to have been under the age of 18 when the crime was committed. Since 1988 it has been deemed unlawful to execute those under 16. While the US signed the International Covenant on Civil and Political Rights in 1992, which outlawed the death penalty for those under 18 at the time of the offense, it reserved the right to execute juveniles. Fifteen states prohibit the execution of anyone who was under 18 at the time of the offense. Since 1990 six countries have executed prisoners who were under 18 when they committed the capital offense. America condemned ten to death; the other five countries are Iran, Nigeria, Pakistan, Saudi Arabia, and Yemen.

The condemned might be innocent. One report claims that as many as 350 people convicted of capital crimes between 1900 and 1985 in America were innocent. Some prisoners escaped execution at the 11th hour, but 23 are believed to have died.

Legal loopholes can win a reprieve at the last minute. Equally there are technicalities which seem to fast-track prisoners to execution.

Death row in Texas is in the "Terrell Unit," named for Charles T. Terrell Sr., a past chair of the Texas Criminal Justice Department and erstwhile supporter of the death penalty. But a letter published in Dallas in February 2000 revealed that even he has doubts:

"We now have an option of life without the possibility of parole.... I think the specter of life without parole... is much more frightening than death by injection.

"Racial disparity is a legitimate issue to investigate. And I believe that anyone facing the death penalty should have the right to a complete investigation as to whether DNA evidence can double-check our legal system for error. Not doing so is a criminal act by society."

A VIEW FROM DEATH ROW

Many criminals condemned to death in the USA are never executed and spend the rest of their days in jail. Others leave death row, for freedom or execution, by quirks of justice.

Napoleon Beazley, a juvenile offender on death row in Texas, sometimes gets letters from children asking what its like in jail. "I tell them to envisage themselves being locked in their room…. No school is allowed, no cassettes or CDs, no computer, so definitely no e-mail. And imagine your mom lets you out in the backyard to play for two hours every day but afterwards it's back to the bedroom…. Throw 400-plus guys in there with you and add fights, killings, stabbings, and while you're at it you can add the fact that the system is all eager to stick some poison in your arm to kill you—that's prison."

The torturous mind games that are played on death row are illustrated in numerous cases. Eric Clemmons was given a death sentence in 1987 for a murder that took place in a Missouri prison. When all his appeals appeared to have failed, Clemmons called his mother to arrange his own funeral. However, new attorneys sought a fresh trial, at which Clemmons was acquitted in three hours. He was the 86th person released from death row in the US since 1973.

In 1999 Anthony Porter was within hours of execution in Illinois before trainee journalists at Northwestern University proved his innocence. Another man has since confessed to the crime. Darrell Mease was saved from execution thanks to a timely visit by Pope John Paul II to St Louis, Missouri where he branded the death penalty "cruel and unnecessary."

In December 1999 David Long was flown from a hospital in Galveston, where he had been on a life support machine following a suicide attempt, to jail—so his death sentence could be carried out.

DAMNED BY LIE DETECTOR

When doubts lingered over the guilt of Roger Coleman in Virginia, 1992, he was offered a lie detector test. The test deems a steady heart rate and normal blood pressure to be a sign of truthfulness. Coleman was given the test on the day he was due to be executed. His heart rate and blood pressure were racing, thus he was judged to be lying. He was electrocuted that same day.

While 50 women were on death row at the time of writing, only four have been executed since 1976. In February 2000 grandmother Betty Lou Beets died by lethal injection, having killed her brutal husband following a lifetime of abuse.

Sister Helen Prejean works as a spiritual advisor to the condemned in Louisiana's Angola prison. After being confronted with the angry family of a murder victim, she began working with those bereaved by violent murder. She wrote about her experiences in a 1993 book, "Dead Man Walking," which was released as a movie in 1995.

A witness at several executions, Sister Helen explains her fundamental belief in the UN's Universal Declaration of Human Rights: "It says that there are two basic rights that can't be negotiated, that governments don't give for good behavior and take away for bad behavior. That's the right not to be tortured and not to be killed."

One New York Senator, James Donovan, made a tongue-in-cheek pro-death penalty comment when he asked, "Where would Christianity be if Jesus got eight to 15 years with time off for good behavior?"

With far greater sensitivity, James Park, a former execution officer at San Quentin, provided an appropriate reply: "As I read the New Testament I don't see anywhere in there that killing bad people is a very high calling for Christians. I see an awful lot about redemption and forgiveness."

ABOVE: Helen Prejean's work as a spiritual advisor was dramatized in the 1995 movie *Dead Man Walking*, starring Sean Penn and Susan Sarandon.

LEFT: Sister Helen Prejean believes torture and execution are against the Universal Declaration of Human Rights.

DEATH ROW, ASIA

On February 5, 1999 Leo Echegaray was executed in the Philippines. Convicted of the rape of his stepdaughter, he was the first person to receive the death penalty there since 1976.

The Filipinos have long wrestled with the specter of capital punishment. The option had not been used for a decade before a 1986 Bill of Rights introduced by President Corazon Aquino outlawed capital punishment. Approximately 500 prisoners on death row had their sentences commuted.

However, almost from the day of abolition, the government was under pressure to revert to capital punishment, mostly engendered through fear of rising crime rates. The death penalty was re-introduced to the Philippines in 1994. Opinion polls suggested strong public support, despite stalwart opposition from the Roman Catholic Church in this traditionally devout country.

Cameramen jostled for position as the condemned man was led to a newly built death chamber at New Bilibid Prison, Manila. Leo Echegaray clutched a Bible and wore a badge which read "Execute justice not people." He and six others were executed in the ensuing months, but to mark the millennium a moratorium on executions was announced on March 24, 2000.

In Indonesia, death row has a remarkable number of political prisoners. Political opponents to the country's government seem to form the highest proportion of those who have died before the nation's firing squad. Sometimes the penalty has been carried out years after the trial.

ELIMINATING DEATH ROW

In Japan there are approximately 50 people on death row. Until recently their identities, whereabouts, and the date of the executions were kept secret. Deaths by capital punishment were reported only as statistics in an annual report.

The justice ministry explained the secrecy protected the survivors of violent crime and shielded the families of the condemned from shame. After criticism from human rights groups, the Japanese government agreed to investigate the issue.

In Communist Vietnam the courts can impose the death penalty for a wide-range of offenses, including embezzlement and damage of state property.

The criminal proceedings in China are largely a closed book to the West. More people face the death penalty in China than anywhere else in the world, and there's a worrying trend of abandoning death row in favor of immediate execution.

During 1996, during a clamp-down on crime, there were numerous radio reports of criminals being found guilty in court and immediately led away to meet their fate. In Jilin province one man, Tian Xiaowei, was found guilty of stabbing a policeman and faced a firing squad within a week of the crime.

Condemned prisoners may be paraded at rallies called by the authorities to highlight a strong response to crime. Usually their hands are tied behind their backs, their feet are shackled and a rope hangs around their neck. The crowd generally respond with approval.

In a grim postscript, human rights groups believe that the organs of executed prisoners are sold to Asia's wealthiest patients for transplants. This has been strongly denied by China's Ministry of Justice.

DEATH FOR ELECTRONIC CRIME

As the last millennium closed, the death sentence was passed on two brothers convicted of computer hacking in China. They had transferred cash from a major Chinese bank into their private accounts. The death penalty was applied to electronic crime for the first time, despite the recovery of all cash involved.

RIGHT: In China prisoners facing the death penalty are shackled when they appear in public. Since the mid-1990s a drive against rising crime rates has pushed up the number of executions.

DRUG OFFENDERS AND THEIR FATE

Travelers gullible enough to carry a stranger's belongings across national borders in Asia are risking their lives. Governments in the region have a hard line against drugs; anyone caught in possession, even unwitting, inconsequential couriers, faces the death penalty.

In the West, offenders are generally viewed as innocent until proven guilty. In some parts of Asia, this ideal has been turned on its head. In Malaya and Singapore, for example, those found in possession of drugs are assumed to be guilty of trafficking. The onus is on the individuals to prove their innocence, rather than on the state to find evidence of guilt. As the offense carries the death sentence, it lends immense urgency to the cause of the accused, who is not best placed to gather evidence on his or her behalf.

Drugs are easy to plant on unsuspecting victims. If possession alone is sufficient to indicate guilt, people are at risk of being set up by love rivals, business competitors, or even the police. Circumstantial evidence carries great weight in drug-trafficking cases, otherwise it would be almost impossible to secure convictions.

Dealers are unscrupulous in their search for couriers, as numerous naïve travelers have discovered. They will pay handsomely when they can persuade people to cross international borders carrying drugs caches. Sometimes they convince fellow travelers to take charge of their bags by way of a favor.

It cost a Thai woman, Navarant Maykha, her life. Aged 32, this ill-educated mother of two was persuaded to carry a bag from Bangkok to Singapore by an acquaintance. She was told the bag contained clothes. When she was arrested at Changi airport in Singapore, officials found 7lb of heroin sewn into its lining.

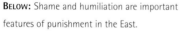
BELOW: Shame and humiliation are important features of punishment in the East.

AT THE MERCY OF FOREIGN JUSTICE

Maykha's pleas of ignorance made no impression on a judiciary determined to stamp out drug abuse. The Singapore government, like the big league drugs barons, was largely unconcerned with the fate of the small fry. She was hanged on September 29, 1995.

Numerous foreigners who have found themselves arrested and charged with drugs offences in the region who, like Maykha, are at a huge disadvantage. Because of the language barrier, most arrested do not understand the accusations of their interrogators, the content of any confessions they are expected to sign, and the proceedings of the court, where adequate translators may or may not be provided. The likelihood of a miscarriage of justice seems enormous.

Countries in Southeast Asia have legitimate concerns about drug-trafficking in their territory. They are in the vicinity of "the Golden Triangle"—Laos, Burma, and Thailand—renown for its opium production. Typically, surrounding countries have small populations and proportionally large numbers of drug addicts.

In Singapore anyone convicted of importing or exporting even a small amount of drugs faces a mandatory death sentence. According to Amnesty International information, of the 349 people executed in Malaysia between 1970 and March 1996, the majority were drug traffickers. In China, one internationally earmarked Anti-Drugs Day was marked by the execution of more than 230 people.

While an unyieldingly strong line against drugs is undoubtedly necessary throughout the region, the governments involved have not addressed the fact that capital punishment is no proven deterrent.

ABOVE: Convicted drug smugglers are paraded in public before being executed in China.

STATE-SPONSORED TORTURE

The Universal Declaration of Human Rights, a benchmark for decency everywhere in the modern world, prohibits coercion by law enforcement officers, yet torture is still applied.

The Declaration states "No one shall be subjected to torture or to cruel, inhuman or degrading treatment or punishment," but distasteful practices still happen worldwide. Undemocratic countries are most prone to abuses during interrogations.

In the past prisoners have often been scarred from beatings; today, electric stunguns are favored, since they leave their victims unmarked. Amnesty International believe that such devices were used in approximately 50 countries during the 1990s. A pulse from a stun-gun is sufficient to cause intense pain, loss of muscle control, and convulsions, but few international controls exist to keep them out of countries with histories of civil rights offenses.

Amnesty International has long been concerned about the abuse of human rights in Saudi Arabia, although the United Nations Commission on Human Rights apparently no longer scrutinizes events there. It is one of the countries where amputation is still considered a legitimate punishment. A convicted offender is likely to lose a right hand for theft and a right hand and left foot for highway robbery.

A film recently smuggled out of Iran reveals that young men found guilty of theft have their fingers amputated by a small guillotine. The same film showed a man having his eye put out.

BELOW: At the Tuol Sleng death camp, members of the Khmer Rouge tied victims to bed frames until they confessed.

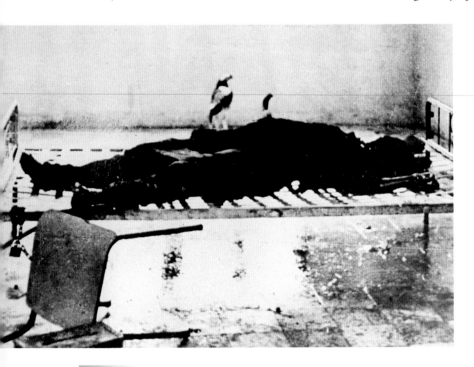

In Saudi Arabia the lash is still used. One Filipino, Donato Lama, was arrested for taking part in a Roman Catholic service in Riyadh. He was sentenced to 18 months in prison and 70 lashes:

"They tied me to a post. My hands were handcuffed and they also shackled my legs....The whip was one and a half meters long [4.5 feet]... with a heavy piece attached to the tip. It was terrible. I would fall when the whip reached my feet but the prison guard would raise me up to continue the whipping. I was amazing to find myself still alive after the 70th lash was given." Afterward Lama received no medical assistance.

WHATEVER INSPIRES FEAR

Throughout the 20th century troublesome prisoners have been committed to mental asylums or hospitals as a more subtle method of torture. Inevitably the mental health of the

ABOVE: The tortures applied under the command of Pol Pot in Cambodia are shown in the country's Museum of Genocide.

internee is chronically undermined. In Cambodia under Pol Pot and the Khmer Rouge, victims held at a torture camp were chained to bed frames until they agreed to sign bogus confessions. As recently as 1999 a Chinese dissident was incarcerated in a mental hospital in Henan province.

Other techniques used worldwide are worthy of the darkest of inquisition cells. In Bolivia the police use *la campana* (the bell), a metal container placed over the head of the victim. The bell is repeatedly beaten; the clamor and vibration are torturous.

In Syria there have been reports of the "German chair," which piles pressure on the spine when a movable backrest is lowered. Detainees in Chad have had cords tied around their heads and tightened with sticks, in the same manner as the garrote, causing bleeding and unconsciousness. Victims in Myanmar (Burma) have been terrorized by a "helicopter ride," in which they are hung by wrists or ankles from a ceiling fan and beaten while it rotates.

The words of French philosopher Montesquieu, who died in 1755, now appear strangely prophetic: "So many men of learning and genius have written against the custom of torturing criminals, that after them I dare not presume to meddle with the subject.... It might be suitable for despotic states, where whatever inspires fear is the fittest motor of government."

CHAIN GANGS

With slavery abolished, a source was still required for free, menial labor. For members of chain gangs, the days were long and tough, and even the Supreme Court could not end their toil forever.

Forced labor was nothing new in America. For years the British used America as a penal colony, until transportees were finally replaced by slave labor. When slavery was abolished in 1865, convict gangs once again came into vogue.

Some southern states began leasing jailed men to independent contractors to work in chain gangs. Manacled together, the prisoners undertook hard labor under the watchful eye of guards. They were employed in road building, agriculture, and mining.

Men were bothered by the indignity of their situation as much as by the heat and the persistent flies. Their plight was illustrated in the Oscar winning 1967 film *Cool Hand Luke*, starring Paul Newman. Based on a book by Donn Pearce, it tells the story of a rebel prisoner working on a chain gang who is finally broken by his brutal treatment.

In 1910, in recognition of prisoners' rights, the US Supreme Court ruled that state laws allowing chain gangs were unconstitutional. However, chain gangs were re-introduced for a third time in 1995, specifically in the groundbreaking state of Alabama and, later, Arizona. In troops 400 strong, the prisoners of Alabama worked 10-hour shifts doing menial tasks, like picking litter from highways and breaking rocks for roads around state prisons.

Proving that crime and punishment are areas of equal opportunity, the authorities in Arizona used women in chain gangs. Dressed in orange and chanting military-style, the women from Estrella jail in Phoenix spent seven hours cleaning up a local neighborhood. Most were happy about being outside—the alternative was spending 23 hours per day in their small cells.

It was branded a publicity stunt on the part of Sheriff-in-charge Joe Arpaio. Despite criticism, he remained unequivocal: "I want everyone to see this chain gang and say, 'That prison is a very bad place to be'."

PRESERVING PUBLIC SECURITY

Opponents are quick to point out that the worst offenders—maximum-security prisoners—are not included in chain gangs. Placing medium- and low-risk inmates in shackles is poor reward for their good behavior.

In 1999 the chain gangs once more disappeared from view in Alabama. It wasn't qualms about human rights that brought about its demise this time. Cuts in public funding left the prison service short of men to supervise the gangs.

BELOW: In Arizona members of chain gangs, like this female group, wear distinctive uniforms when dispatched onto the streets to undertake community projects.

ABOVE: The monotonous hard labor that chain gangs have to do is intended to defeat the mind as well as the body.

China has used convict labor for years to forge ahead with public works. Figures are sketchy but insiders have estimated that 16 million prisoners work on production lines in farms, factories, and within prison camps. A further six to eight million do hard labor.

The Communist regime offers plenty of scope for gathering the necessary manpower. By far the largest numbers of those detained and tried are dubbed counter-revolutionaries. The penalty is "reform through labor," which may take place at any one of the 155 prisons, 492 rehabilitation centers, or approximately 40 social integration centers for juveniles.

Hard labor became a common feature of the so-called Cultural Revolution. The aim was not just to break the body but to mold the mind. Reading matter, even conversation, was strictly controlled.

China's Deng Xiaoping defended the system: "Under the present conditions, using the suppressive force of our nation to attack and disintegrate all types of counter-revolutionary bad elements, anti-party, anti-socialist elements, and serious criminal offenders in order to preserve public security is entirely in accord with the demands of the people and with the demands of socialist modernization construction."

BLOOD MONEY

Imagine that a relative was murdered and the killer caught and brought to justice. Would you demand a life for a life? Or would money be enough to resolve your grief and spare the murderer?

I slamic law permits blood money to be exchanged for a condemned prisoner's life. It means the next-of-kin of a victim of crime may accept a cash payment from the accused. The victim's relative is deemed compensated, and the life of the accused is spared.

In Saudi Arabia, a man was pardoned when his family agreed to pay 2.3 million riyals (US$613,000) to a murder victim. Through the payment of blood money, two British nurses linked to the murder of a third in Saudi Arabia in 1996 escaped harsh penalties.

Deborah Parry and Lucille McLauchlan were arrested after the battered body of Australian Yvonne Gilford was discovered. Both signed confessions that they later retracted, claiming they had been beaten into submission. Nevertheless, Parry was believed to have been sentenced to death and McLauchlan to 500 lashes in court proceedings in Saudi that were veiled in secrecy.

At first it seemed Gilford's brother Frank was unmoved by the plight of the nurses. He believed them guilty and thought they would face justice. However, he was ultimately persuaded to accept a substantial settlement after British businesses raised money after an appeal by the families of the nurses. Frank Gilford kept a nominal sum to cover his expenses and gave the remainder to an Australian hospital.

Deborah Parry and Lucille McLauchlan were released in May 1998, following a pardon granted by Saudi's King Fahd. They had spent 16 months in a cramped and insanitary women's prison.

MONEY NO COMFORT

Of course, the bereaved family may reject the blood money and not show clemency for the accused. In Afghanistan in 1997 a soccer stadium was packed with some 10,000 spectators who gathered as the fate of convicted murderer Abdullah Afghan hung in the balance.

Afghan had been tried and sentenced by the Islamic High Court of Kandahar. An appeal to the ruling fundamentalists Taliban Supreme Court was rejected. The judge, traveling in a four-wheel-drive pick-up and speaking into a microphone, arrived at the pitch to lecture the crowd for an hour on the intricacies of Islamic punishment before pronouncing the death sentence.

Then the judge turned to the relatives of the murder victim and appealed for them to accept blood money. "You will go to Mecca ten times if you spare this man. Our leaders have promised to pay a huge sum to you from the Baitul Mal [Islamic fund] if you forgive him."

The relatives would not be moved. Afghan was hauled from another pick-up, shackled with chains and shaking with fear. He was taken by guards to the goalposts at one end of the stadium, where he said a final prayer. The guards handed a Kalashnikov rifle to an avenging relative who raised it and fired three times at Afghan's back. When his body flopped backward, the armed man fired another three bullets into the chest.

RIGHT: Lucille McLauchlan and Deborah Parry were spared the punishment set down by a Saudi Arabian court when blood money was paid to the victim's brother.

PRISON CONDITIONS

A vicious fight between rivals gangs is nothing new. But American TV viewers were shocked to discover a clash they saw was in a state prison and apparently instigated by warders for their own amusement.

Corcoran state prison in California—home to notorious prisoners including Charles Manson and Sirhan Sirhan, assassin of Robert Kennedy—has earned a reputation for violence since it was built in the late 1980s. Seven prisoners were shot dead by warders in the first few years of the Nineties and a further 43 were injured, earning it an unenviable reputation. It was claimed that guards staged gladiatorial contests, placing bets on the outcome.

Investigators found it difficult to bring errant warders to justice. A code of silence extended to both prisoners and officers. Five officers were persuaded to speak out about the fights between prisoners, during which officers may have taken the opportunity to kill inmates. The prison authorities have acknowledged racial tensions; Corcoran has abandoned its integrated yard policy, in which inmates of different ethnic backgrounds exercised in the same area.

Prisoners in the USA and Britain are paid for menial work they do while behind bars. The cheap rates paid to convicts, substantially lowering the cost of contracts, has sparked a row in America over the ethics of pitting prisons against factories, which must meet bigger wage bills. The subject becomes considerably more contentious in the case of privately run jails.

In Scandinavia prisoners are given more demanding jobs, with greater wages and other benefits. Sometimes they get a form of parole as a reward for their labor. America has experimented with conjugal visits for inmates in which they and their partners are given access to a trailer. This "bonus" is already open to prisoners in Scandinavian countries.

No deterrent

The United States has the highest incarceration rate in the world. The United Kingdom puts a bigger proportion of its population behind bars (nearly ten percent—64,000 prisoners) than any European country except Portugal. The British prison service is burdened with a high number of jails built in the Victorian era, which drags standards down. Slopping out—the practice of emptying a bucket used overnight as a toilet—still exists in many British prisons, and cells often hold more prisoners than their intended capacity. These poor conditions have led to riots.

Prisoners are constantly moved between jails, particularly if there are fears that a power-base or personality cult is being established among inmates. After a jail-break from Britain's Whitemoor prison, it was found that terrorist prisoners were pampered by guards and, by common consent, "ruled the roost." Other headline-grabbing problems are the widespread use of drugs and the number of suicides.

Rehabilitation is generally reserved for juvenile criminals who are placed in young offenders' institutions, away from the malevolent influence of older prisoners. The idea that adults have a fervent desire for productive lives after a spell behind bars has largely been abandoned. Experts in criminology now accept that inmates are not deterred by the prospect of prison. The rate of re-offending is approximately two-thirds, which may be higher than for those who are not jailed at all.

More than two centuries after John Howard, the great prison reformer, published his recommendations to cure the appalling conditions in English prisons, there are still giants steps to be made. The problem of violence among inmates remains endemic. Conditions are not always sanitary and warders are not necessarily honest or even humane.

LEFT: Strangeways in England is one of several British prisons where poor conditions have caused the inmates to riot. In this rooftop protest a dummy in jailers' clothing is hanged.

BELOW: Alcatraz, infamous island prison and archetypal example of the US penal system, now acts as a tourist attraction.

LYNCHINGS

Lynchings were all too common in America's Deep South for some 70 years. The victims were often hanged without trial—or even after being found innocent.

The term "lynching" is believed to come from Charles Lynch, a magistrate who permitted punishments of British Loyalists during the American Revolution without recourse to law. Lynchings became a feature of frontier life when pioneers found themselves miles from the nearest sheriff or courthouse. With the American Civil War they became associated firmly with black people, although errant whites still incurred the wrath of the mob.

Between 1880 and 1920 more than 5,000 black Americans were lynched in the southern states. The peak year was 1892, when 230 allegedly occurred. Researchers have realized that this coincided with a drop in the price of cotton, when whites felt threatened. Georgia and Mississippi had the largest numbers of lynchings; none have occurred in the six New England states.

BELOW: This early lynching was in protest at the British taxes the victim had enforced in colonial Boston.

In 1901 Congressman and former slave George Henry White proposed a bill that would make lynching illegal. He told fellow Congressman that of the 109 people lynched during 1899, 87 were black. The bill was swiftly defeated.

Dr Arthur Raper produced a damning report on lynching 30 years later. "Practically all the lynchers were native whites. The facts that a number of the victims were tortured, mutilated, dragged or burned suggests the presence of sadistic tendencies among the lynchers. Of the tens of thousands of lynchers and on-lookers, only 49 were indicted and only four have been sentenced."

However, a reporter for *The Chicago Chronicle* in 1897 believed the lynch mob's "sole offense consists in having done the right thing in the wrong way."

A lynching was held to be so respectable that people from all classes, white women and children would boldly gather around to witness the event, despite its unlawful nature. It was not uncommon to sell sections of the rope afterward.

PROVOKED BY REASON

Racism inspired and supported the lynch mobs. Parallels have been drawn between the Nazis treatment of Jews and the southern

ABOVE: This imprisoned man had the body of his alleged murder victim tied to him; a worse fate has arrived in the form of a lynch mob.

American approach to blacks. There was no reasoning with a lynch mob, which numbered anything between 50 and 500. Pleas for mercy fell on deaf ears. With the apparently unassailable strength of a lynch mob, whites created a powerful psychological fear in the black community. Some historians have gone so far as to insist that it is the terrorist tactics of lynching that maintained black oppression and white supremacy for so long.

While some lynchings were of people found guilty of a crime, others occurred before a trial had taken place. Those declared innocent after a trial might still be hauled off for lynching. Ironically, fair-minded citizens who overtly ensured a balanced trial often outraged the mob and provoked a lynching.

Although slavery was abolished following the American Civil War, the black community found little sympathy among southerners, who feared black freedom. Poor white tenant farmers found themselves in competition with newly freed blacks and sought ways to feel superior. Politicians seeking popular support indulged in racist speeches that rallied public anxieties.

The Ku Klux Klan tried to manipulate the mobs. Created in 1866, disgruntled whites turned to the organization after the Civil War. KKK members were recognizable by their white robes and pointed hats. Their "calling card" was a burning crucifix. Although it was officially disbanded in 1869, the KKK had largely achieved its objective of imposing white rule in the southern states.

The Klan was revived in 1915 but within 20 years its membership declined. It has spawned numerous groups still in existence, but these are weak and fragmentary.

CONCENTRATION CAMPS

*Concentration camps should not be thought of as the domain
of Hitler's Germany. Spain used them in Cuba during the
Spanish-American War in 1898, and Britain expanded on
the concept during the Boer War.*

Britain entered the Boer War in 1899 to defend the rights of foreign miners with the misguided assumption that the conflict "would be over by Christmas." When Britain unexpectedly suffered a string of defeats, their army supremos—including Lord Kitchener, who was to find fame in the First World War—decided to round up Boers.

As able-bodied men had been recruited to fight against the British, women and children were predominantly taken, along with an estimated 115,000 black workers. Taken by force by British soldiers, the last glimpse most had of their farms or homesteads was masked by smoke. A "scorched earth" policy was in action, intended to deprive the fighting Boers of food and shelter.

The Boers spent some time surviving in the open before marching or traveling in cattle trucks and railway wagons to the 45 camps, which were typically established at inhospitable sites. The British preferred to call them refugee camps, but the presence of barbed wire fences and armed guards betrayed their aim. Boer families were to be confined as part of a military strategy.

Concentration camps differ from jails in that inmates do not face criminal proceedings, yet they are incarcerated for an unspecified period. Generally, the camp commanders call the shots, rather than government or civil authorities.

Conditions for the 136,000 Boers were dreadful. To prompt the surrender of those still free and fighting a guerilla war, the rations were halved; small children starved as a result. There was little by way of sanitation, which soon led to widespread disease. Doctors and nurses were few.

ABOVE: David Lloyd George (1863–1945) campaigned against British use of concentration camps during the Boer War.

VICTORY BY NEGLECT

Many people slept on bare ground, even during the winter months. Humane internment requires months of preparation and investment, something that simply never happened in South Africa. Research indicates that the refusal to supply necessary medical aid and sufficient food was a deliberate policy pursued by Kitchener and others when they were unable to secure victory in the field.

There was an outcry in Britain and overseas. Future Prime Minister Lloyd George said, "The fatality rate of our soldiers on the battlefields, who were exposed to all the risks of war, was 52 per thousand per year, while the fatalities of women and children in the camps were 450 per thousand per year. We have no right to put women and children into such a position."

British journalist W.T. Stead wrote: "Every one of these children who died as a result of the halving of their rations, thereby exerting pressure onto their family still on the battlefield, was purposefully murdered."

By the end of the conflict more than 28,000 Boers had died, along with 17,000 blacks. The plight of the black Africans was widely ignored until a cemetery containing the bodies of victims was recently discovered.

Britain had similar camps, albeit with better services and provisions, during both World Wars to hold anyone with German links. Explorer Sir Vivian Fuchs, who brought glory to Britain in Antarctic exploration, was brought up in just such a camp on the Isle of Man because his father was German.

In the United States during the Second World War, some 42,000 people of Japanese extraction were removed from their homes on the west coast—thought to be at risk from invasion—and held in camps with a further 70,000 people drawn from all over America who were considered enemy sympathizers.

LEFT: Boer women and children suffered terrible deprivation in camps like this one in the Transvaal.

BELOW: A view of Auschwitz, which developed into a death camp in Nazi territory.

GULAGS

If Russian prisoners of war thought the worst was over following liberation by victorious Allied forces in 1945, they were sorely mistaken. They were sent to work camps every bit as bad as the Nazi's.

At the end of the Second World War, Soviet authorities sent Russian ex-prisoners of war to gulags—labor camps in remote regions of the USSR, notably Siberia. They were suspected of having collaborated with the enemy. These were the very men who, next to Jews, had been most loathed by the Nazis. Some soldiers, suspicious of the intentions of their leader, Stalin, vanished from holding camps all over Europe before they could be dispatched to their fate.

Gulags existed before the war and would busily continue for years after. Their existence is overshadowed by the Nazi labor camps. Gulag history is not as faithfully recorded, relying mostly on the writings of survivors like Alexander Solzhenitsyn and facts that have spilled from the Kremlin since the fall of the Iron Curtain.

Siberian prisons were not Stalin's invention. He was detained in such camps twice by the Tsarist regime before the Bolsheviks took control. When he gained power in Soviet Russia, Stalin had two pressing problems: he wanted to industrialize his country, fast, and he had a sizeable population of kulaks—landed peasants—whose resources he desired.

BELOW: Laborers from a gulag contributed toward the Soviet industrialization program by building a canal.

In simple terms, his solution was to send kulaks to gulags, where they could work toward industrializing the country, leaving Stalin to grab their meager wealth. Once the kulaks were dealt with, he found no shortage of people to suspect of treason, sabotage, and the all-encompassing "anti-Soviet agitation and propaganda." Some were accused by family and friends. Most confessed after brutal interrogation. They were deported from their homes, thousands of miles across this enormous empire, into a harsh reality they were unlikely to survive.

CLIMATE OF FEAR

In 1937, in an estimated 700 camps, the gulag population was thought to be between five and six million. The survival rate was 10 percent.

The gulags were not extermination camps in the same sense as Auschwitz—although there was an execution program in Soviet Russia—but people died in their thousands. They died from hunger and cold. Some died of exhaustion, driven to construct buildings, dig canals, or work in mines. Their quarters were insanitary, thus disease was rife. The rape of women inmates was common. Sadism by the guards accounted for some deaths.

Though the guards treated prisoners abominably, they too were victims of the Soviet propaganda machine. They apparently believed without question that prisoners were likely to bring down the state, blow up factories, abuse children, and so forth. There was the unspoken threat that guards who objected to the way prisoners were treated would join the unfortunates on the wrong side of the wire.

A strata of authority lay below that of the guards. Hardened criminals established their own power bases and heaped abuses on the political captives.

ABOVE: Stalin was once held captive in a Siberian prison.

LEFT: An abandoned Siberian prison camp, where countless people died in misery.

The misery of the gulag is revealed in the following verse sung by internees:

I will die
They will bury me,
And no one will know
Where my grave is.
No one will go there,
No one will come,
Only in the early spring
The nightingale will sing.

DISRESPECT FOR THE DEAD

Before a victim of the gulags was disposed of, guards often drove a pickax through their skull. Some bodies were buried in mass graves blown out of the Siberian ground with dynamite. Others were dropped through holes in the ice that covered nearby rivers; during the spring thaw, the bodies were washed into the Arctic Ocean.

WAR CRIMES OF THE SECOND WORLD WAR

Since 1864 wounded soldiers and prisoners of war have been protected by the Geneva Convention. This international agreement aims to safeguard men who fall into enemy hands but has been broken numerous times.

I t is impossible to dwell on the Second World War without considering some of the appalling abuses of the Geneva Convention. The killing of hundreds of Polish men at Katyn Wood, near Smolensk in what was then the Soviet Union, became a notorious example.

Invading Germans discovered the bodies in February 1943, after being tipped off by local peasants. In radio bulletins the Nazi regime pointed the finger at Stalin and his Bolsheviks. The Soviets hit back, claiming "The Hitlerite murders will not escape a just and bloody retribution for their bloody crimes." It was only in 1990 that Russia's President Gorbachev released documents from the NKVD, the Soviet secret police, that proved Stalin's elite were behind the atrocity.

BELOW: Identifying the dead at Katyn Wood was a terrible task. German soldiers were accused, but it was later admitted that Stalin's men committed the atrocity.

The Poles had been captured when Soviet forces spilled over the Polish border. A short-lived agreement between Hitler and Stalin drawn up in 1939 permitted the division of Poland between the two powers. Approximately 230,000 Polish fighters fell into Soviet hands.

Presumably on the grounds that they were class enemies, Stalin ordered the deaths of the 4,143 men killed at Katyn Wood in 1941. Others were slaughtered at different sites in the Soviet Union.

The Poles had been told they were heading home. Before being hauled from the train that transported them from prison camps, they were filled with apprehension. "Optimistic as I was before, I am now coming to the conclusion that this journey does not bode well," wrote Waclaw Kruk in a diary found near his body.

At Katyn Wood each man was bound by a rope before being dispatched with a shot to the back of the head. The stacks of corpses were covered with lime and sand was bulldozed on top.

A RUTHLESS AGENDA

In France the cruelty of the Nazis is epitomized by the fate of Oradour-sur-Glane. In one summer's afternoon in 1944 the population was eliminated by a vengeful German SS. Men were herded into a barn and shot. Women were locked into the village church, which was then set alight. Children were sent to concentration camps. Explosives reduced the village's 250 buildings to rubble. Before the day was over 642 residents of Oradour were dead. The few survivors were badly injured and psychologically scarred.

ABOVE: Survivors from Oradour-sur-Glane testified at the war trial.

The reason for the massacre can only be guessed. At first it seemed the villagers were victims of a savage reprisal for French Resistance activity. Later it was claimed that German commanders were looking for a stash of loot that they had amassed but lost to a Resistance ambush.

The German SS was also guilty of excesses against Allied troops. On December 17, 1944 one hundred American troops were killed near the Belgian town of Malmedy during the Battle of the Bulge, Hitler's last gasp of the war. The Americans were trapped by a surprise German attack led by Major Joachim Peiper.

After a brief spat the GIs surrendered. They were disarmed and placed in a field under armed guard, forced to watch the enemy surge ahead, until someone barked an order—"Machen alle kaput" (kill them all).

The firing continued for three minutes. Those that survived slid under the prone bodies of their comrades and feigned death. They heard the SS walk among the Americans, finishing off the wounded with shots to the head.

WAR CRIMES IN ASIA

The Japanese sought death and glory, hence the kamikaze suicide attacks of pilots who flew into approximately 40 US warships in 1945. Surrender was a matter a great shame, so their ethics were challenged when thousands of enemy troops gave themselves up.

ABOVE: An estimated 10,000 men died on the march from Bataan after the fall of the Philippines.

W ith its lightning war in Southeast Asia in the months following Pearl Harbor, Japan gained many new territories and thousands of prisoners— American, British, Australian, Dutch, Chinese, and Korean—who had surrendered when hope was lost. The Japanese were mentally and physically unprepared by this deluge of men. Japanese culture dictated that Allied soldiers were cowards and nowhere in the campaign of aggression was there a facility to accommodate prisoners. Accordingly their response to the captives was unrestrained and barbarous hostility.

Americans and Filipinos rounded up when the Japanese overwhelmed the Philippines were forced to march for 60 miles from Bataan without adequate food, drink, or rest.

An estimated 10,000 men died on the march through dense jungle, from a total of 75,000. At their destination, Camp O'Donnell, conditions were poor, food was sparse, disease was rife, treatment by guards was vicious—and four out of ten died within the first three months.

The Japanese hierarchy soon realized the benefits of a large, cheap, expendable workforce. The men captured in the fall of Singapore were soon ferried north to work on the notorious Burma railway, furthering the Japanese ambition of invading India. Japan had signed the international convention, which expressly forbade the use of prisoners of war in projects that would assist their enemy, yet still Allied men became their slaves.

BOUND BY THE JUNGLE

Many of the prisoners came via Changi, a massive camp in Singapore where conditions had appeared squalid. After traveling for days in steel rice railway trucks to camps hewn out of virgin jungle, Changi began to seem like paradise. Before leaving Changi, they were compelled to sign a declaration that they would not attempt to escape. Again, this flew in the face of international law.

The prospects for escape were grim. Few men gave themselves a hope of survival in the jungle, and if they were caught the penalty was death. The skill of

RIGHT: The Santo Tomas University Internment Camp in Manila was home to some 400 prisoners-of-war. They existed in primitive conditions and, with little medication, many succumbed to jungle diseases.

the firing squad was woefully lacking—an Australian was left unscathed, after numerous rounds had been fired. "For God's sake, shoot me through the head and kill me," he roared.

Shocking stories of appalling brutality and sadism by the Japanese guards became known after the war. They threw boulders at men working below, forced prisoners to push enormous rocks up steep hillsides, beat men, threatened and caged them.

Out of 60,000 Allied prisoners, an estimated 12,000 died. Of about 270,000 slave laborers drawn from China, Burma (now Myanmar), and surrounding countries, there were 70,000 deaths. At the end of the Second World War, the British alone hanged 265 Japanese for their cruelty, but this has done little to soothe the fury of veterans.

A POW's VIEW

In his book, "The Night of the New Moon," writer and philosopher Sir Laurens van der Post describes his experiences as a captive of the Japanese: "I had been made to watch Japanese soldiers having bayonet practice on live prisoners-of-war, tied between bamboo posts, and had been taken to witness executions of persons of all races and nationalities for obscure reasons like showing a spirit of willfulness or not bowing with sufficient alacrity in the direction of the Rising Sun."

JUSTICE AT NUREMBERG

When Hitler was at the height of his power, Nuremberg was a magnificent medieval city that bore testimony to his appeal with a series of stunning rallies. With a sense of dignified irony, the Allies held the momentous trial of the most significant Nazi war criminals in Nuremberg's Palace of Justice in 1945.

BELOW: The Nuremberg trial draws to a close; the Nazis now know their fate. (Front row, from left: Hermann Goering, Rudolf Hess, Joachim von Ribbentrop, Wilhelm Keitel; row behind, fourth from left: Fritz Sauckel.)

B y war's end Nuremburg was no longer the picturesque heartland of the Third Reich—Allied bombing had reduced its prestigious façades to rubble. The trial was not a triumphal showpiece, rather a way of closing a miserable chapter and turning the page for a fresh beginning.

In the dock at the International Military Tribunal were 20 men from the upper echelons of the Nazi regime, among them Luftwaffe chief Hermann Goering and the Führer's deputy Rudolf Hess. Martin Bormann was accused in his absence. Robert Ley, Director of the Labour Front, hanged himself in his cell before the trial opened.

They faced four charges: conspiracy, crimes against peace, war crimes (including shooting prisoners of war), and crimes against humanity (including the Holocaust). The USA, Britain, France, and Russia had prosecution teams at this unique courtroom occasion. Eight judges heard the evidence.

Chief prosecutor Robert Jackson began proceedings on November 20, 1945 with the words: "The privilege of opening the first trial in history for crimes against the peace of the world imposes a grave responsibility. The wrongs which we seek to condemn and punish have been so calculated, so malignant, and so devastating, that civilization cannot tolerate their being ignored, because it cannot survive their being repeated." The Allies, he said, had stayed "the hand of vengeance" and submitted to law.

It took nearly a year to complete the hearing. It was largely a formal, ordered affair, with the defendant sitting impassively listening to each case through headphones.

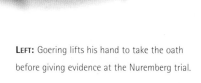

LEFT: Goering lifts his hand to take the oath before giving evidence at the Nuremberg trial.

GOERING ESCAPES THE NOOSE

By October 1, 1946 a dozen men who a few short years before were at the peak of glittering, although tarnished, careers were told they were to hang. Six others got jail terms of between ten years and life, including Hess, who died in Spandau Prison, West Berlin, in 1987. A further three were acquitted.

On the morning of the hangings—October 16, 1946—Goering's body was discovered in his cell. Anxious not to be hung, a fate he considered shameful, the corpulent *bon viveur* had swallowed a cyanide pill.

One by one the accused filed to a gallows in the prison gymnasium in Nuremberg. Each man mounted 13 steps to meet the noose, but each had a different response. Streicher shrieked "Heil Hitler" with his last breath. A smile played on the lips of Hans Frank, a convert to Catholicism. Keitel's last thoughts were with Germany's war dead: "More than two million German soldiers went to their death for their fatherland. I follow now, my sons—all for Germany." Both Ribbentrop and Seyss-Inquart, the first and last to be executed, expressed hopes for future peace.

It was by no means the only trial of war criminals, but it was the most significant and cathartic. Other trials took place consecutively and in the following years, throughout Germany and also in Japan, China, and the Soviet Union. At Nuremberg, the Subsequent Proceedings lasted until the end of 1948 and dealt with a further 182 war criminals. Of those, 26 faced the death penalty.

EXECUTED AT NUREMBERG

Hermann Goering; Martin Boorman; Hitler's foreign minister Joachim von Ribbentrop; armed forces chief Wilhelm Keitel; Ernst Kaltenbrunner, chief of the security police; Alfred Rosenberg, the wildly anti-Semitic party philosopher; Hans Frank, head of the Polish territories; Wilhelm Frick, Nazi party boss; propagandist Julius Streicher; Fritz Sauckel, in charge of slave labor; strategist Alfred Jodl; Artur Seyss-Inquart, Reich Commissioner for the Netherlands.

ETHNIC CLEANSING

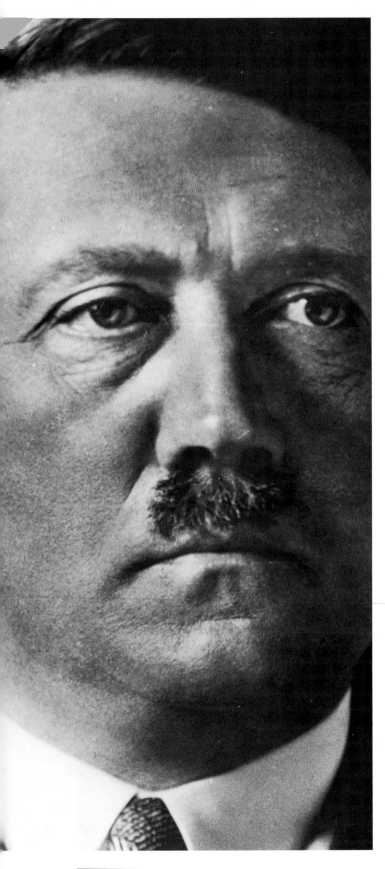

Ethnic cleansing—a clinical-sounding term for the eradication of a particular nationality or culture— became the crime that tainted the 20th century. The perpetrators included the infamous dictators Adolf Hitler, Pol Pot, and Saddam Hussein.

The torture and execution of thousands of people, victims merely because of their beliefs or birthright, leaves us wondering how it could happen. Perhaps Stalin had the answer when he observed that one death was a tragedy; a million deaths were merely statistics.

While the wholesale killing of Jews was not new (see page 55), Hitler gave anti-Semitism new currency with the Holocaust. In turn he inspired other despots to mimic his grand plans, although each had a pet "enemy" earmarked for extinction.

Hitler tapped into an anti-Jewish swell prevalent in Europe in the later 19th and early 20th century when Jews were perceived by some to have a greater slice of wealth and power. His hatred of Jews was no secret. Philosophies of anti-Semitism, nationalism, and the superiority of the Aryan (white) race were written as early as 1923 and ultimately appeared in *Mein Kampf*, which sold more than five million copies and made Hitler a millionaire. Persecution of Jews became accepted.

Hitler established concentration camps soon after he came to power. The first, at Dachau, Buchenwald, and Sachsenhausen, housed not only Jews but Communists, criminals, Jehovah Witnesses, gypsies, homosexuals, dissident Nazis, and political opponents of all colors. Inmates worked in dreadful conditions for the benefit of the Reich. Concentration camp population stood at some 50,000 by the outbreak of war and rose sharply afterward. Conditions deteriorated.

In 1935, two years after becoming German Chancellor, Hitler drew up the Nuremberg Laws, which effectively withdrew Jews from German citizenship, drove them from public life, and confined them to sordid ghettoes.

NIGHT OF THE BROKEN GLASS

On November 9, 1938, domestic anti-Semitism reached a crescendo in the Kristallnacht or "Night of the Broken Glass." More than 170 German synagogues, along with 7,500 Jewish stores, were destroyed by rampaging Nazis, in reprisal for the assassination of a German official in Paris.

"Incited to a pitch of insanity, the mob vented its emotion on defenseless people," said German diplomat Hans Bernd

Gisevius, an opponent of Hitler. Still, there was no internal backlash against the regime, even when it declared that the Jews had to pay for the damage they "provoked" and were deprived of insurance money.

It wasn't until 1941 that Hitler vocalized his desire for a "final solution" to the Jewish question. Consequently, the Wannsee Conference was held early in 1942, where it was agreed that "Europe will be combed from west to east" for Jews who would be duly worked to death or immediately killed. The first gas chambers were installed within months and death camps were established in Poland.

Survivors and liberators concur that conditions in German camps were abominable. People were crammed into primitive huts infested with vermin, with poor sanitation. A diet of thin soup with small portions of bread was insufficient to fuel inmates who faced grueling daily labors. They were subject to arbitrary acts of sadism by the guards. Most died within a matter of months.

When the British entered Belsen they found 10,000 unburied corpses. Stripped of all self-respect, the frail inmates were like shells, incapable of emotion. They were dying at a rate of 500 per day.

Colonel Vassily Petrenko, a Red Army liberator of Auschwitz, reported "I saw starving people who looked like shriveled mummies. I saw the instruments of destruction used against them and realized that this was not war but a crime against humanity."

ABOVE: Jews and others considered enemies of the state were taken to concentration camps. An extermination program instigated in 1942 claimed the lives of millions.

LEFT: Hitler made his anti-Semitic views clear in his book, "Mein Kampf," written in 1923.

ABOVE: A wall of the Museum of Genocide is lined with portraits of prisoners who died under the Khmer Rouge.

POL POT'S ANTI-CAPITALIST REGIME

Following the Second World War, the United Nations outlawed genocide, significantly toughening international laws on the issue. One of the most tragic aspects of the appalling episode is that mass killings were repeated time and again in the remaining years of the 20th century.

One of the most prominent offenders was Pol Pot, head of the Communist Khmer Rouge party in Cambodia. His regime came to power on April 17, 1975, when youthful soldiers wearing black pajama suits and red scarves took possession of the Cambodian capital Phnom Penh.

Pol Pot was born Saloth Sar in about 1925 to a peasant family in the Kompong region of Cambodia. His left-wing tendencies crystallized when he studied electronics in Paris in 1949. On his return to Cambodia in 1953 he devoted himself to building a revolutionary group that was radical even in Communist terms.

Having overthrown the government, Pol Pot instituted some of his policies. To wipe out capitalism, he chose to delete industrialization in favor of a strictly rural economy. The entire population was forced from urban areas into the countryside, where they would work as peasant slaves. The evacuation was at gunpoint. No one had the opportunity to refuse—those that did were shot or clubbed to death. The elderly and the sick fell by the wayside on the forced march. Orphaned babies were left to die in hospital cribs.

Instead of 1975 it was Year Zero, denoting the fresh start. Books were burned, schooling was banned, and money was abolished. Cambodia became Kampuchea. All ties with the outside world, save China, were severed.

PARANOID OF INTELLECT

But Pol Pot knew that he would be unable to sweep away the memories that people held of the years of freedom prior to his takeover. Scientists, doctors, lawyers, teachers—anyone with a vested interest in returning to a balanced regime—appeared to be his greatest threat. His answer was to exterminate them, by the thousand. Anyone who betrayed a morsel of education was hauled off and killed. Wearing spectacles was enough to condemn a person to death.

Cambodia had its "killing fields," where bodies of the dead were dumped in putrefying heaps. Those who escaped the counter-revolutionary accusations of the arrogant young soldiers and suspicious comrades were at risk from starvation, for the economy crashed along with production rates and there was insufficient food to go around. As many as two million died in the four years that the paranoid Pol Pot was in power.

Three Westerners were tortured and executed in 1978 after they were captured while on vacation in Thailand. Before his death, Englishman John Dewhirst "confessed" that he was an American agent who had attended a CIA school and that his father, a headmaster, also worked for the CIA.

By 1979 neighboring Vietnam had been provoked once too often by border skirmishes and invaded Cambodia. Afterward, Vietnam's foreign minister Nguyen Co Thach admitted, "We did not go into Cambodia to save them. We went there to save ourselves. But what we found shocked even us who have seen so much war."

Pol Pot and his men retreated into the hills, where they continued using terror tactics. Ironically, they received both Chinese and Western backing. Pol Pot died in 1998, his final years shrouded in secrecy. The Tuol Sleng torture and death camp, where victims were chained to bed frames until they signed bogus confessions, became a Museum of Genocide.

ABOVE: Pol Pot was inspired by left-wing philosophy. From a committed socialist he became a genocidal leader.

TRAPPED IN THE IRAN-IRAQ WAR

The first recorded instance of genocide in the 20th century was the killing of up to 1.5 million Armenians by Turks, during and after the First World War. Armenians are a highly developed people with an ancient culture who lived in significant numbers in Turkey. A surge in nationalist feelings—viewed very much as a threat by the host nation—was sufficient to inspire the killings.

Further south the Kurds, a Moslem people living within the borders of Iraq, Iran, Turkey, and Syria, have been subject to shocking massacres during later years of the 20th century. They too seek a homeland, but their nationalist sentiments are not appreciated, particularly by the Turkish and Iraqi governments.

Kurds living in the city of Halabja were felled in thousands as Iraqi leader Saddam Hussein authorized the use of chemical weapons against them in 1988. Iraq was at war with its neighbor Iran and the border city, at the heart of the war zone, decided to pitch its lot with the Iranians. Before Iranian troops could defend the city and Saddam Hussein wreaked terrible revenge for the "betrayal."

Early on March 17, 1988 the Iraqi air force exploded cyanide, nerve and mustard gas bombs. Those killed by the cyanide dropped where they stood, strangely unscarred. Nerve gas causes suffocation, its victims wearing a contorted death mask. Mustard gas chokes and burns, leaving those afflicted with skin peeling away like paper. At least 5,000 people died that day, and the final death toll has been put as high as 15,000.

ABOVE: Thousands died after Saddam Hussein experimented with gas attacks on the border city of Halabja in 1988.

CONFLICT IN THE BALKANS

When Western observers entered Halabja less than a week later, they were horrified. One UN official said: "The bodies were lying in doorways, in streets, around tables set up for lunch and in cellars where people mistakenly sought shelter from the heavier-than-air gas. Many other corpses were found on the roads leading from the town, where residents had failed to outrun the spreading cloud. The victims seemed to have died quickly, as there were few signs of a struggle. The streets were also littered with the bloated carcasses of cows, dogs, cats, sheep and goats."

Perhaps the most heart-rending sights were of the men who were working in distant fields when the gases were unleashed. They returned to find their entire families wiped out.

Despite international condemnation, Saddam was prepared to use gas warfare against civilians again. Later the same year, Butia was among a clutch of Kurdish villages wiped out. Many of the agents needed for the manufacture of the gases had been supplied by Western businesses with the blessing of their governments.

Dark murmurings of ethnic cleansing were heard in the 1990s, when the Balkans were rent apart by strife. Enmities in the region stretch back to the 14th century, when Serbs were defeated by the Islamic Ottoman Empire. Serbians continued to quest for a homeland and the freedom to follow its Orthodox faith.

GENOCIDE IN AFRICA

Ethnic cleansing has not been a European preserve. In Africa, for example, there were massacres in the devastating conflict between Nigeria and Biafra in 1969. More recently, accusations of genocide have passed between the rival Hutus and Tutsis in Rwanda.

Although the Serbs were given satisfaction by 1881, they had to face numerous enemies, not least the Croats who by the Second World War aimed to force Serbs to convert to Catholicism. This troubled history led to a three-cornered fight in the region, which tore entire communities to shreds. The millennium closed with conflict in Kosovo, in which Serbians tried to rid the region of Albanian Muslims.

ABOVE: An attempt by Serbians to oust Muslims from Kosovo erupted into a vicious conflict involving soldiers from all over Europe and international peace-keepers.

CONCLUSION

With a study of torture and execution behind us, it is time to look toward what the future holds. Public opinion in America seems to be veering away from the death penalty, which is encouraging. However, as the 21st century begins, there is worrying evidence that the road to a civilized society will remain long and fraught with problems.

The persecution of Christians in Japan has long since ended. They are no longer lowered on a rope into the mouth of the volcano Mount Unzen to die in its burning sulfurous fumes, as they were in the early 1600s. Yet persecution of numerous faiths still exists around the world.

"Running the gauntlet" is no longer used as a punishment in the armed forces. This barbaric ritual forced the victim to walk between two columns of men armed with clubs, birches, and the like and suffer their blows. It often ended in death. Yet news of similarly abusive initiation rituals are still commonplace.

New technology has given fresh inventiveness to the realms of torture and execution. In Columbia guerillas glued an explosive "necklace" around a 53-year-old-woman. It decapitated her, killed a bomb disposal expert who was trying to free her, and blew the arms off two soldiers who were assisting him. The guerillas picked her for punishment simply because she refused to meet demands for cash.

A SYMBOL OF HOPE

Across the Atlantic in Africa rebels in Sierra Leone hacked the hands from government supporters after President Tejan Kabbah campaigned with the slogan: "The future is in your hands." One of the youngest victims was nine months old.

In Saudi Arabia the largest execution in 20 years took place when seven Nigerians were beheaded for their part in an armed bank robbery. Three more had their right hands and left feet amputated. All these dreadful events occurred in the first months of the new millennium.

Italy has made positive links between the old world and the new. The Colosseum, symbolic of a violent past, was illuminated with bright white lights before the 20th century ended. These lights will change to gold when any convict is spared execution or if a country abandons the death penalty.

The Italian government, the Vatican, Amnesty International and the United Nations made the bold abolitionist statement because they see parallels in the modern world to the way emperors used gladiatorial exhibitions to deflect public criticism. We continue to strive for a humane response to human weakness.

GLOSSARY

Archaic Period ancient Egypt between c.3100 and 2755 BC.

Ba human-headed bird that in ancient Egyptian times was thought to represent the essence of the human soul.

bastinado Chinese bamboo cane usually used to beat the bare feet or buttocks.

Bedlam Bethlehem Hospital, an early home for the insane.

benefit of clergy in a time when only the clergy and a select few could read, being able to recite from the Bible (the 51st psalm in particular) would reduce the severity of a criminal's punishment.

Bloody Codes 18th century laws based on the Waltham Black Acts of 1723, which dictated the death penalty for more than 200 offenses.

brazen bull hollow wooden bull that was burned with a victim inside, their cries transformed with a system of pipes.

canque type of portable pillory used in China until the 20th century (also called the *tcha* or *kea*).

crouched burial rare method of Anglo-Saxon interment in which the body is placed in a crouching position in the grave.

Danelaw Viking law once imposed across much of northern and eastern Britain.

equuleus Roman instrument of torture over which a victim was stretched with weights.

First Fleet the ships carrying troops and convicts that landed in Australia in 1788 to build a penal colony.

flagellum Roman whip used for flogging.

flax plant, the fibers of which are used to make linen thread; its seeds are pressed for linseed oil.

brank metal headgear with a strap that gagged the wearer to stop them talking (also known as the scold's bridle).

garnish bribery to prison keepers.

garrote a Spanish device that strangled or broke the spine of the victim; early versions consisted of a rope pulled tight around the neck, later twisted tighter with a stick, and more sophisticated versions screwed a piece of metal through the top of the spine.

gibbet scaffold or cage upon which the bodies of the dead were displayed.

Hanging Match hanging day.

Iron Maiden a coffin or sarcophagus with spikes on the inside too short to rapidly kill the person confined within.

Ka A spirit-partner; ancient Egyptians believed the body's soul, or *ba*, would re-unite with its *ka* on death.

Kenbet regional high court of Ancient Egypt.

kia quen Chinese foot-crushing torture instrument.

knout Russian whip.

kulak derogatory term for wealthy Russian peasant, literally translated as "the fist."

ling chi "Death of a Thousand Cuts"—Chinese execution method in which flesh is sliced off the body to prolong a painful death.

mabinogi 11th-century Welsh prose based on older oral stories.

mazzatello a mallet used in Italy to smash the victim's skull; the throat was usually cut soon after.

Mosaic Code specific criminal offenses and defined punishments as set out in the Old Testament.

Ordinary clergy for convicts.

quaestio Roman court licensed to oversee torture sessions with the aim of extracting confessions for use in evidence.

saga Viking eulogy to a mythological or historical hero.

scavenger's daughter a large hinged metal circle used in Tudor England; the victim knelt on it and had the upper half of the circle pressed against their back (also called "Skeffington's gyves").

scurvy disease caused by lack of fresh fruit and vegetables causing swollen joints, sore gums, and body weakness.

Seru counsel of elders in ancient Egypt.

suttee the Hindu tradition of a wife sacrificing herself on the funeral pyre of her deceased husband.

tean zu Chinese torture where wood is placed between the fingers and the entire hand tightly bound.

Thing a Viking court.

triple tree a three-cornered crossbeam at Tyburn, England's hanging capital until 1783, that could hang 24 people at a time.

turned off pushed off a ladder to hang.

virgin's kiss wooden model of a woman, studded with spikes, which could be pressed into a victim's body as a form of torture or execution.

wheel victims were tied to the rim of a large, wooden, horizontal wheel and beaten with a metal bar; the wheel was then propped upright.

wickerman a large wooden cage in the shape of a man, filled with people and animals, then set alight by Druids.

INDEX